I0160744

YIELD
* * * * FOR * * * *
ONCOMING GREATNESS

CAPPING CAPITALISM

Matt N. Tabrizi

Thinking Hat Press

#YFOG

Please use #YFOG on social media for news on
Yield for Oncoming Greatness: Capping Capitalism

Thinking Hat Press
Yield for Oncoming Greatness: Capping Capitalism
Matt N. Tabrizi

Copyright © 2015 by Matt N. Tabrizi.
All Rights Reserved

Copyeditor: Lindsey Alexander
Cover Design: Cyrus Tabrizi
Interior Design: Kevin Callahan / BNGO Books

All rights reserved. No part of this publication may be reproduced in any form or by any means without written permission from the author. For permission, please contact us at http://yfog.us.

Published in the United States by Thinking Hat Press
ISBN: 978-0-9962100-0-3
Version 1.1 (Blueberry)
Printed by CreateSpace

MY THANKS

To the one, who let me be,

To my mother, who gave me life twice,

To my father, who taught me right from wrong,

*To my wife Aurea, who has been my North
Star and supporting companion,*

*To Cyrus and Kayvon for giving me hope
and being all a father can ask for.*

*My family is part of everything I do, and this work is no
exception. Cyrus designed many great covers until this one took
the spotlight. Kayvon went above and beyond any expectations,
by providing invaluable critique and the perspective of a
bright young adult. Aurea encouraged me to write the book
and helped me at every step of the way to see it through.*

My sincere thanks and eternal love.

Contents

★ ★ ★ ★

Note

Asterisks (*) represent references, which are available at the end of the book as well as online at yfog.us/ref.

The Land of the Free

★ ★ ★ ★

When the sliding glass door opened, I reflexively took a step or two backward. The hot, dry weather in contrast to the cool indoor air of the Dallas airport was just unexpected. After a momentary pause, I continued. I had just arrived from London with no particular plans or intentions. The thought that there would be no return through these doors had never crossed my mind.

I had lived in London for the past year, but otherwise I had spent all my twenty years in my native country of Iran. Coming to the United States was a sudden decision that I had made only the previous day. In fact, I was not coming to America; I was running away from my life in London.

Like most middle-class or upper-class Iranians at the time, I could have run away to any country, but I would not have considered going to just any country. There were only a few countries that we Iranians would have considered living in or possibly calling home. The US was at the top of that list, with the UK a distant second, followed by other European countries. This is despite the facts that the US was an ocean farther away than Europe and that Iran had just undertaken a revolution to live free from American influence.

Although most Iranians would not easily admit it, I, like many of my countrymen, looked up to America despite its role in restricting our country's freedom. Perhaps we viewed Americans much as we saw our ancestors who, as a powerful force, created an empire while remaining just. After all, Cyrus the Great went down in history not only as the ruler of the largest empire the world has ever seen but also as the creator of the first human rights charter. By means of such a comparison, we could reconcile America the all-powerful and America the land of the free.

As a typical Iranian teenager, I was fascinated by technology. I remember reading, back in the 1970s, an article in the *Daneshmand* (The Scientist) that described a high-tech US military satellite. According to the article, this orbiting satellite could zoom in and determine whether one had shaved in the morning! There was no disputing America's superiority in the military sector, in science and technology, or in the economic realm.

America's power was easy to perceive and understand. But America as the land of the free was and is an abstract idea for Iranians, and perhaps for billions of people in many other countries around the world. We had lived and been raised under the Shah's dynasty, whose intelligence service, Savak, was notorious. We understood that we were "free" as long as we followed a defined path; hence, freedom was an abstract idea. To use an analogy, imagine that you are a bird born in a cage inside a windowless room in a castle. All your life you long to be free, but what does it mean to be free? For you, freedom means flying about and exploring the windowless room, and nothing more. You are unaware that there is a castle beyond the room and a universe beyond the castle. We were the bird, and the room was our understanding of the land of the free.

A few years after my arrival in the US, I was driving back from the beach with a friend. I heard sirens and saw a police car in my rearview mirror. The policeman stopped me and issued me a ticket for speeding. I signed the ticket, thanked the officer, and I took off. Half a mile later, the policeman stopped me again—apparently I had taken off a bit too fast. He came to the window and asked if I was a diplomat. I said no and asked why. He explained that only a diplomat might risk getting a second ticket without caring. While I was not a diplomat, in my young mind a speeding ticket meant only a monetary fine to be paid. He promptly wrote me another ticket. I signed it and thanked him again. He asked if I was heading back home to Virginia and I replied yes. He said, "Please follow me. I will escort you out of Delaware to ensure that you stay below the speed limit." And that is what he did.

Here was a policeman, representing the power of the state, interacting with a foreign national who seemingly did not respect the law. Yet the officer offered help, thus ensuring that the law was respected. To me, this version of freedom was way beyond the windowless room and the castle.

Living under the dictatorship of a mighty king has its benefits. One of them is a deep suspicion of any plan, good or bad, big or small, executed by the government or an individual.

This suspicion leads to an openness toward conspiracy theories, such as the theory that the British and American governments conspired against Dr. Mosaddegh, an Iranian leader who attempted to establish a democratic government in 1953. That idea, once a conspiracy theory, is now known to be a historical fact.* Another benefit of living under a dictatorship is that one develops an acute ability to discern and measure the erosion of freedom.

Three decades after my arrival in Dallas, I have gone far beyond the castle and fallen in love with freedom and the land of the free. I have no conflict about my nationality or my origin. I am a proud American citizen and this is the land of my children. At times, though, I wonder if my children know there is a universe beyond the castle. A few years after 9/11, on a flight returning from Cancun, I asked the American flight attendant if she could ask any of the passengers to accommodate my family so that we could sit together. She promptly said no. I sarcastically replied, "Thank you." Sensing the sarcasm, she said, "Would you like me to throw you off this plane? You know I can." To which I responded, "I know you can," and sat down.

Most Americans' idea of dictatorship includes visions of armed guards and roadblocks, or the inability to travel or publish, as portrayed by Hollywood. These ideas are occasionally accurate, but they are extreme forms of dictatorship, exercised only when absolutely necessary. During the Shah's reign, we traveled, talked, gathered, and published as we pleased. We rarely saw guns or guards. In fact, none of our American acquaintances at the time would have recognized a dictatorship. Iran appeared as free as any

Western country. That freedom was superficial, however. Most people never dared to say what they thought or to publish anything contemptuous. The only criticism of the government was in the form of entertainment—that is, it was embedded in the soap operas and nightly shows designed to act as a relief mechanism. There was an invisible yet solid and clearly understood line that no one would cross. Anyone who did criticize the government was labeled a communist, and the Iranian society had no more tolerance for communists than we Americans have for terrorists today. In the US, the mere accusation of being a terrorist can practically ruin one's life, even if the accusation is proved to be false. Although we are justified to have zero tolerance for terrorism, we have to be cautious of an atmosphere that shifts the emphasis from the act to the label.

Compare my experience of getting a speeding ticket (even two of them) to my experience with the flight attendant. The difference between the two is the difference between being free and not being free. When issuing the ticket, the officer made no assumptions about me, except that I was guilty of speeding and that I may be indifferent about getting tickets, even though, as a police officer, he represented the power of the state. On the other hand, the flight attendant was to provide my family and me with a service that should have contributed to both my convenience and my safety. Yet knowing to what extent the state would allow her to abuse her position, she simply and not so subtly reminded me that all it would take to get me thrown off the plane would be for her to claim that I said the wrong word, looked the wrong way, or acted in a suspicious manner. By the time I would have recovered from her accusation, it would not have mattered whether I was guilty or innocent. This is a state of suspicion and paranoia rather than a state of democracy and freedom. A basic form of freedom is to be treated as innocent until proven guilty. How did you feel the last time you passed through airport security?

Back in Iran, my father was a well-connected and religious merchant. My mother was also religious, with most of her family serving in the military, including my uncle, who was the head of the Green Berets. So I grew up knowing God, money, and connections. As such, my experience as a youngster was not biased toward any one of these to the exclusion of the others. I recognized the value of all three.

Since the beginning of my professional career, I have been building companies. I understand deficiencies and what must be done not only to fix these companies but improve them. I see no difference between building a family, a company, and a country, except that, in the case of a country, the scale of the work required is much larger and many more people are needed to get it done. I was recently forced off the board of my own company, which shows that making a difference is neither easy nor always possible. Fortunately for me, it also means that I finally had time to finish this book, whose original title I conceived several years back during the housing market crash.

As you read through YFOG, you will see that I raise many issues and present a solution for each one. My purpose is not to provide an in-depth analysis, which is what my critics would claim is needed. While their criticism may be valid, I would point out that we have been debating some of these issues for decades with no result and that perhaps it is time for an alternative approach. Additionally, there are already great books, which my readers can follow up with, covering most of these topics. To achieve greatness, though, I believe that we must demand changes in many areas. A colleague of mine said that it would take several years to become an expert in solving a single one of these issues. He implied that I should not attempt to solve these issues. By extending his argument, no one should attempt this and expect to improve all aspects of our society. That was his true belief, however, that philosophy leads to inaction, the status quo, and a society not governed by its people. In short, he implied that the average person does not understand what needs to be done. I believe that while an average person may not understand, most men and women recognize a problem and if a solution to it works. We all know these problems exist and that we need to fix them. Deep in our heart, we also know what needs to be done. My suggestions are intended to be catalysts and fire starters. This book takes a common-sense approach to the issues. As you read, let your common sense dictate whether these solutions are sensible.

America, like ancient Persia, has been a lighthouse and a refuge for many around the world—a sanctuary for Jews, Christians, and Muslims alike. We have a duty to ourselves, our children, and all the birds in cages around the globe to bring America back to its glory and once again make it the country that others look up to. YFOG is not about America's foreign policy, but about threats to America from within. YFOG is about us. It is about the steps I would take to keep the lighthouse shining if I had a magic wand. It is about keeping America the land of the free. These are the views of a traveler who has enjoyed capitalism, experienced dictatorship, and adored the land of the free, but who fears the future of the world his children live in.

I may not have a magic wand to make the changes I am suggesting, but I believe that collectively we are the magic wand. We, taking responsibility as individuals, while acting collectively, have the power to change anything and everything. I also believe that we need this change, we want this change, and we must change.

INTRODUCTION

Perceptions

★ ★ ★ ★

We walk through life seeing what we see and acting as we act, believing that others see and act in the same way. Yet, in reality, we are all driven by our perceptions. We perceive life through our individual lenses, which have been crafted through our experiences, our background, and our upbringing. In short, all of us view the world through our beliefs.

It's 1983. The long white ceiling is frequently interrupted by bright white lights as I am carried on a stretcher. I feel some pain in my fingers as they hit the side of the fire doors, but I am unable to move them. In fact, the only body parts I can move are my eyelids. A few minutes later, I am hooked up to an intravenous dialysis machine. Twenty minutes into the dialysis, a vein in my arm bursts and blood gushes everywhere as in a horror movie. My sister passes out and hits the floor. Two nurses hold my arm and apply pressure on it as they attempt to stop the bleeding. Blood is all over me, on the nurses, on the floor, and in the tubes. But I am alive.

A few hours later, it's six in the morning and I am in a room at Behavard Hospital, Tehran's center for kidney treatment and dialysis. The doctor comes in. He is the same doctor who saw me in the back of a cab the night before, just outside the hospital. And he is the same doctor who told me to go home and return in the morning. I ask him why he sent me home, and he replies that he did not think that I would have made it and he did not want to add to the hospital's mortality rate. I feel that I have cheated death.

A week later, I am in London, receiving a live kidney from my mother. I stay with my cousin and his wife, to whom I will always be indebted for treating me so wonderfully. While there, her sister joins us. We spend lots of time talking in their small flat or across the street in Regent's Park. Over the months, we realize we have a lot in common despite our different back-grounds—and we fall in love. We decide to get married, so I contact my brother-in-law, my godfather, to follow our tradition and ask her parents for their blessing. In the meantime, her mother arrives in London. She, of course, is unaware of our feelings for each other and apparently has someone else in mind for my loved one. Although we do not have prearranged marriages in our culture, it is common for courtship to begin with the blessing of the parents. Almost overnight, our world crumbles and we find ourselves in a no-win situation: I have to choose between following my heart or being ungrateful to my hosts and leaving with a broken heart to avoid conflict. I choose the latter and buy a plane ticket for the US. She wants me to stay and work it out, but I leave on the next flight to Dallas. For the next six months, tears are my best companion.

A few years later, I am in my last year of college. I have just spent a month in the hospital. I used to receive money from my inheritance regularly to pay for my expenses, but for the last few months I have not received any, so I am out of money and facing about sixteen thousand dollars in hospital bills. My father left us enough money in properties to live a good life, but I have spent a good amount since his passing and then learn that all remaining properties have become worthless since the Iranian revolution of 1979.

We perceive life through our individual lenses. Suffering a broken heart, losing considerable wealth, and cheating death at a young age bestowed upon me a blessing that I could not have gained by any other means. Most of us live our lives as if we stand on solid ground, on imaginary tracks that will continue forever, whereas in fact everything we have can disappear in an instant, right before our eyes. Every day we see people around us losing their wealth, health, or loved ones due to acts of man or God, but we keep our blinders on and continue living ignorantly. My blessing has shown me our fragility and allowed me to value life, people, and relationships above all else. In ancient Persia, before the arrival of Islam, people followed a simple principle: *good thoughts, good words, and good deeds*. Simply put, be a good person. Life is too short to have it any other way.

We have become a society of slogans and quick fixes. We call blacks African Americans to fix racism. We subject our bags to searches in the interest of public safety, but we do not ask how tons of drugs get into our country. We fight for our right to bear arms to protect our constitution, while at the same time our constitution is being used to protect the rights of mega-corporations against individual citizens.

Our freedom is disappearing right on our watch, and we are too busy debating the same issues in every election: abortion and guns. Although both issues are important, we should not allow them to overshadow other important policies affecting our nation. While there are cases where guns have been used to provide personal safety and protection, there are many safe countries in which guns are illegal. If guns are to protect our freedom, I would like to ask how such usage and an unconditional stance on the right to bear arms have helped our freedom. I would also like to ask those who have been seeking to disallow abortion even in cases of rape or incest whether our country's morals have risen due to this unconditional stand. If I were to draw an analogy, it would be that our Titanic is sinking and we are concerned about our sleeping arrangements.

We live in a world in which our jobs are taken by people living in countries that we cannot identify on a map. We elect presidents only to debate where they were born once they take office. Many of us earn minimum wage, but vote for millionaires to represent our values and address our concerns in Congress. We cannot afford to care for our elderly parents, but we happily provide a lifetime of care for convicted murderers. And the list goes on.

We clearly do not live in the world of our fathers, and we certainly do not live in that of our forefathers. We follow their laws, but not their values. We believe that ours is a complicated world, so we propose to settle for what's most important; yet we are told what is important by the media, which is owned and operated by individuals and corporations who may not necessarily share our values or concerns.

While we debate whether a twenty-first-century woman living in the land of the free should have access to birth control, our freedom gets chipped away, our wages decrease, and our houses are auctioned off and rented back to us.

The world is truly complicated, but our problem is not the complexity of the world. The world of the caveman was just as complicated, relative to his knowledge and abilities, as our world is relative to our skills and comprehension. The issue is perspective and attention. We must sort through the noise, determine what matters, and correct our perspective. We need to understand what is important. Once we do this, we can make critical and significant adjustments.

This book is about compromises. It's about *Yielding for Oncoming Greatness*. It recognizes many shades of gray. It is about making concessions to what we can tolerate, so we are not forced to sacrifice that which we cannot bear to lose. YFOG is not about idealism; it is about solutions that, seemingly too big to be practical at times, are realistic and within our reach, and will restore the land of the free to its glory.

This is what I believe and what we will discuss in more detail in the coming chapters: I believe that our system of capitalism, the concentration of wealth, and income inequality have reached levels for which we are seriously unprepared. We allow capitalism and the accumulation of wealth to be limitless without a clear understanding of its consequences. Few of us really know what a billion dollars is or what that much money can do, yet there are thousands of billionaires, some with hundreds of billions in net worth. I believe that this level of capitalism is the true enemy of our freedom. We need to cap capitalism.

I also believe that moderation is key to all aspects of life, and that extremism must be avoided at all costs. Any form of extremism, whether from the right or the left, and whether it is religious, libertarian, nationalistic, economic, or social, chips away at our freedom. We feel that we have the right to impose our extreme views on others only until we become the recipient of such views. I believe that, except for our creator, nothing is absolute, and attempting to maintain any aspect of our lives in a radical state only creates chaos.

I believe that we should start from within, but fixing ourselves is not a prerequisite to fixing what is around us; we must do both. If a loved one and I are drowning, I do not ponder whether I should save myself or my loved one first. I need to save both. I need to have the desire to live and to love. I must survive so I can save my loved one. These objectives are not different from each other; they are the same. We need to simultaneously fix ourselves and our society in order to achieve our goals. To do so, we must first ensure that our values are right.

For centuries, we have fought to keep our religions, but also to keep them separate from the state. There are countries with great degrees of separation and others where religion and state are inseparable. In reality, there is no proof that one method works better than the other. While I believe that moderate degrees of separation are needed, extremism is a problem regardless of the degree of separation. We need a society that is governed by its people through logic and science, but we equally need strong values, which can be derived from both organized and non-organized religions. My father was a pious man, and he used to say, "If you worship nothing, worship a rock." When it comes to right and wrong, it is not good enough to simply answer to another mortal man, who is subject to the same temptations as we are, and expect to succeed. We need to answer to a higher power, an inner power, in order to walk the right path. We need an absolute power in our lives to empower us, even if it is a rock.

I believe that everyone should pursue happiness, but what does it take to be happy? The top-of-mind answer is typically money, and why not? Money may play a role in our happiness, or more accurately, its absence may play a role in the lack of happiness. However, when it comes to money, the real question is how much is enough. The common answer would be the more, the better. Again, why not? Well, assuming that everyone wants money and lots of it, the problem becomes scarcity.

Scarcity, the fact that resources are limited and that what one takes must be replaced by someone else, is something we like to ignore, as individuals and as a society. But ignoring the laws of the universe does not reduce their effect—gravity pulled on the cavemen as much as it does on modern physicists. Acknowledging and understanding our limits can have an effect on everything we do, from what we say to how much we spend.

One may use the fact that resources are scarce to defend communism, according to which wealth can theoretically be divided among people in such a way that people contribute to the general wealth equally. However, communism defies the human desire to grow, to need, and to own, and for these reasons it has failed. Capitalism, on the other hand, rewards efforts and mobilizes our desire to grow. Sadly, those same desires and traits also lead to abuse, poverty, and inequality.

How much we collectively earn is directly related to the state of the economy and the wealth of the nation. The economy, simply stated, is a function of what we produce, what we spend, and what we invest in our country's future to maintain or increase what we produce. Our productivity is the result of many factors, but in its simplest form, it depends on how much each of us contributes to society. That amount is determined by the number of years we effectively work, how productive we are, whether we mow the lawn or create Google or iPods, and how long we do *not* contribute—i.e., the age at which we begin working and how long we live after retirement. I will address all of these factors.

We must continue to increase our productivity and stop waste, but we also must ensure that every member of our society benefits from our prosperity. This would allow our productivity and GDP to rise further while narrowing the gap between the haves and have-nots. Wealth is never created equally, and I do not expect it to be so, but I suggest steps to address wealth concentration and income disparity. I will also propose various ideas to increase efficiencies and stop waste while increasing the quality of life.

So money does contribute to our happiness in two very tangible ways. First, it pays for our necessities: food, shelter, education, transportation, healthcare, etc. Second, it makes us feel better about ourselves by improving our self-image and self-confidence. Money also makes us feel safe; it allows us to pay for our children's education or take care of ourselves when we retire.

Apart from feeling secure with money or, more accurately, feeling insecure without it, money is a way to take care of things or simply pay the bills. Most of us see this at work every day, but most of us may not give it enough thought. Each month we work, our earnings get deposited into our accounts, and our bills get paid.

So in theory, individuals would need less money for their necessities if society as a whole took care of our common needs. For example, if universities offered free bachelor's degrees in exchange for the funding they receive from the government, I would not need to pay my children's tuition, and if I do not need to pay the tuition, I can pay more in taxes and afford to live with less money. According to this argument, shouldn't society pay for everything so I don't have to? The answer, of course, is no. The justification for society to pick up the tab is not so I can avoid paying my bills. We can justify society paying for those services when a few conditions are met:

First, that a service at a certain level be necessary for our society to function. High school education and interstate highways are good examples. Second, that a service be necessary to everyone potentially, such as Social Security. Third, that only the government can provide such a service, such as the enforcement of national security or border control. Fourth, that it be equally available to everyone, as in the examples mentioned here. Equally available to everyone does not mean equally and directly used by everyone. We all pay for our infrastructure, such as the roads we travel on. Some of us travel and use these roads extensively while others may seldom travel. Nevertheless, we all pay for them.

There is nothing new about this concept. We already pay lots of federal and state taxes to receive these services. I believe that some of these services are no longer adequate, such as a high-school education, which is free and available to all. Others are inefficient, such as the postal service, Medicare, and Medicaid. I will suggest that some services must not only be paid through taxes but also be performed solely by the government—otherwise our freedom may be eroded. Private prisons are an example of such erosion. As members of our society, you and I pay for everything, which means we also pay for inefficiencies, wastes, and unnecessary bureaucracy. We must make changes, but to do so we need to better understand human nature and the sources of influential power, and then make swift and broad changes across our society. The changes that I discuss in this book are of a political, financial, or social nature.

I suggest changes that affect our political system since it controls how one is elected. If we have the right people in office, they will make the right decisions. But we cannot solely rely on politicians or the government to do the right thing; so I will propose that independent organizations help us. We also need help to know what the *right thing* is. I will propose changes to create access to unbiased investigative reporting.

I suggest changes of a social nature, starting with our educational system, and then address a few laws that contribute to inequality and waste. To protect our freedom and democracy, I argue that the police, jails, and the military must not be privatized. Among other issues, I'll address Social Security and retirement.

With the understanding that our resources are limited, I will discuss solutions designed to preserve our nation's wealth, such as changing the monetary system, along with solutions that create efficiencies across our society, such as improving the post office, and suggest ways to repurpose our spending. An example of the latter would be to stop the war on drugs and use the resources saved to declare war on cancer.

In most cases, there is more than one reason to suggest a change, and there is more than one benefit to the solution. Healthcare, on which I will spend relatively more time, is a good example. Changes to our access to healthcare affect us both socially and financially.

Finally, I will discuss our spirituality as a function of living a more satisfying life; our personal responsibilities; and our behavior as a starting point to changing negative social trends.

1

The Tripod of Power

★ ★ ★ ★

U ndoubtedly, the haves have always had power over the have-nots, perhaps as early as the Stone Age. I would think that a man possessing a nice sharp piece of stone could have held some power over one who did not have one. Most likely, as early as the discovery of fire, people realized that if they could control a source of energy, they could use it as a bargaining chip, but this concept did not become practical until the discovery of oil. With the growth of oil as an energy source, the British, and eventually everyone else, realized that if they could control its supply, they could control the world.

Understanding that material, whether oil or a sharp stone, can be used as leverage was simple. What took wit was realizing that one could create leverage by being the middleman who facilitated the trading of such assets. We now know these facilitators as bankers. The other source of power, formalized as early as the Roman empire, if not earlier, is a set of rules that could be used as leverage; hence rulers and their modern equivalents, lawyers and politicians, were born.

In earlier times, most often a single entity or ruler held all these sources of power. These rulers, as still seen in some countries today, set the rules, controlled the supplies of natural resources such as oil, and were rich. Nowadays, the sources of power are less concentrated.

While oil still plays a huge role in geopolitics and wars are still waged to control it, oil is only one source of wealth. Nowadays, huge amounts of wealth may be amassed through virtually any industry. In fact, thanks to the IMF monetary policy, Margaret Thatcher, President Reagan, and President Clinton, as well as the end of the Cold War, global privatization shifted a large amount of resources from the public to private citizens around the globe, and billionaires were born.

In the United States, billionaires were often made through ingenious methods. The Walton family made their fortune by removing middlemen and inefficiencies in the supply chain, allowing them to offer goods to the general public at warehouse prices. Microsoft became the standard for personal computing, and Facebook changed the way people socialize and communicate.

Forbes magazine's 2014 global billionaires list includes over sixteen hundred billionaires with a total net worth of $6.5 trillion.* With so many billionaires, a billion dollars may not seem like a significant amount. After all, if there were over a thousand Niagara Falls, Amazons, or Egyptian pyramids, we would no longer consider them significant. In fact, we would probably turn a dozen of the pyramids into exotic hotels for our entertainment. But in reality, a billion dollars is a monumental amount.

It is difficult to understand a billion. It is an amount too large to be easily imagined or measured. Let's see if we can attempt to get a feel for what a billion is. If you work for thirty years, earn $100,000 a year, pay 30% of your income in taxes, and save the other 70%, it would take you 476 lifetimes to make a billion dollars. In other words, if every generation of your descendants did the same, it would take until 16,300 for your dynasty to accumulate a billion dollars.

If you are in the upper end of the middle class and make $250,000 or even a million a year, it would take 190 or 48 lifetimes, respectively, to achieve the same goal, meaning that your descendants would reach a billion in 7728 or 3443 respectively. Simply stated, whether you make minimum wage or a million dollars a year, you are about the same in the perspective of a billionaire. Here are two other facts to put a billion dollars in perspective. First, if you line up a billion one-dollar bills lengthwise to circle the earth, you would go around four times before you run out of bills. Second, if you earn 5% annual interest on your billion, you would make $4 million a month, $1 million a week, over $5,000 an hour, or $95 every minute, purely from interest.

If we compare the billionaires' net worth to the gross domestic product or the purchasing power of all countries, their aggregate wealth puts them in third place after the United States and China.* If we include the European Union, the billionaires' net worth would be in fourth place. Again, a group of 1,600 people has more purchasing power than every country in the world except for a superpower, a continent-wide conglomerate of nations, and a country with over a billion people. Their net worth is also greater than the combined GDP of 175 countries. There are 489 billionaires in the United States alone, with an aggregate wealth of $2.3 trillion — 14% of the United States' GDP — placing them in the tenth position when compared to the GDP of other countries. Interestingly enough, only one billionaire has made his fortune from law or (more accurately) from lawsuits. However, if we include lending and investment banking within the banking category, there are over 230 billionaires from this sector on the list, responsible for 13% of billionaires' total wealth. The banking category is second only to the goods and services category. There are over 90 billionaires in the energy sector, responsible for 5% of that wealth.

I believe that the accumulation of wealth by billionaires is the largest threat to our freedom and must be tackled as a clear and present danger. This is not to say that there is anything wrong with how they have earned their wealth, or with the billionaires themselves. In fact, two of the top three richest people on the list are Bill Gates and Warren Buffett, who happen to be the most generous philanthropists the world has ever seen. The issue lies with those who do not use their wealth for good causes and with the implications of people having a net worth of over a billion dollars. After all, we did not divide AT&T into the Baby Bells because the company was necessarily doing something wrong, but because it had enough power to monopolize its industry.

So billionaires clearly have the power to tilt the playing field, and they can do so if the law is on their side. That's where politicians come in. Politicians in democratic societies are supposed to be the guardians of freedom. However, if getting into office to serve the country requires millions of dollars, that automatically tilts the political scale toward the rich. There is no dispute that running better propaganda improves the odds of winning, and if more money means more propaganda, then that is yet another advantage for the rich.

But politicians cannot get away with just about anything, as it may seem. They need the public behind them, and that is where the media comes in. An Iranian proverb says, "He who goes to the judge alone wins." In other words, any judgment depends on how the facts are presented. The media plays an enormous role in shaping public opinion. Consider O.J. Simpson, whose case started the phenomenon of real-time news sensationalism.* Most of us believe that O.J. was guilty of the alleged murder charges against him, even though the court ruled that he was innocent. This may not be the best example, but it demonstrates how our opinions on various issues are based on the information we receive.

An even better example, perhaps, is Saddam Hussein's alleged collection of weapons of mass destruction (WMDs). We were told that he possessed them and that he denied having them. We invaded Iraq, and after the damage was done, we discovered that there were never any weapons of mass destruction in the first place. Considering that Iraq has the fifth largest oil reserves and twelfth largest gas reserves in the world, one can speculate about the situation in a different light: politicians needed to invade Iraq, so they used the media to mislead us with the excuse that Iraq had WMDs. The rest is history. This theory is, of course, difficult to prove, but if it were true, it would be an example of how the rich, through politicians, use the media to control energy. I believe that billionaires, politicians, and the media are the sources of power in today's society. I call them the tripod of power.

When talking about the rich we must not forget that there are also mega-corporations with much more wealth and power than some billionaires. However, such corporations typically have shareholders and a board of directors, and in the US, their actions are subject to more rules and scrutiny than those of individual billionaires.

The billionaires clearly present the largest threat to our democracy, the media can frame our view of any issue and can help or hinder any candidate, and the politicians can implement the billionaires' agenda. This is a tripod of power because each leg needs the other two in order to stand. To ensure that this tripod of power does not adversely affect our democratic society, we need to tackle politicians, then the media, and finally, the billionaires. Making these changes will not happen quickly and may seem impossible at times, but our nation is known for accomplishing the impossible. We have done it before and we'll do it again, but to do so we must unite as a country, and in order to unite we must compromise; for greatness, we must yield.

2

The Financial Transparency Service

★ ★ ★ ★

The largest spender in every economy is the government, and the American government is not an exception. In 2014, it spent $3.5 trillion.* This is a huge number, but in and of itself the amount does not tell us much. We enjoy the largest economy in the world with a GDP of $16.8 trillion, so government spending is expected to be in the trillions. Our government spending and budget are not secrets and are openly discussed, budgeted, and reported. The real question is how easily we can access these numbers and how detailed and transparent they are.

When we know what happens to our money, it leaves less room for abuse and corruption. To know what happens to our money, I suggest a system called the Financial Transparency Service (FTS), for the purpose of ensuring transparent financial reporting that is easy to understand

and accessible by all US citizens. The FTS would show where the government's money comes from and where it goes. Money is a powerful incentive to do good or evil. If its flow is transparent, the people can ensure that it does more good than evil. While we cannot expect the FTS to be used in the private sector, we should expect it to be fully implemented in the government and in government-related entities, including government contractors and subcontractors, to the extent of their contractual relationship with the government. The FTS would also apply to tax-exempt organizations that do not pay their share of taxes. Similarly to the government, non-profit organizations' financials are publicly available. Organizations such as Foundation Center (foundationcenter. org) make access to non-profit entities' tax filing much easier. The available information, however, does not really reveal enough details about their financials. To arrive at my point, look up the DC chapter Red Cross' filing.* You will see that not much is revealed in these filings, and to get more details one must spend a great deal of time and effort. The FTS makes the financials of non-profit organizations, not just their tax filings, readily available. In short, if an entity uses taxpayers' money or doesn't pay its share of taxes, its financials must be open and visible to the public. That is what the FTS does.

The Financial Transparency Service will be available via public websites and apps, and an API (Application Programming Interface, which allows one program to interact with another) should be available to developers for use within their applications. The FTS would also standardize and simplify accounting jargon so it can be understood by those without a degree in finance or accounting.

The FTS would provide plug-ins for various accounting software used by the public and private sectors. These plug-ins could allow entities to continue using their various accounting systems while providing information to the FTS.

For easy access, I propose the implementation of a website dedicated to the FTS. The site would be maintained by a group of accounting volunteers within the Freedom Watch group, which I discuss in a later chapter. This group will carry out financial reporting, assign and maintain the reporting hierarchy classifications, add new organizations, and, most importantly, flag discrepancies.

The site would be relatively simple. It would consist of simple graphical reports combining P&L (profit and loss, which shows where the money comes from and where it goes) into a balance sheet (list of assets and liabilities). The reporting hierarchy would allow users to view reports at a general level and obtain more specific details that are necessary for financial transparency.

This does not mean that the government cannot keep secrets or a private budget for intelligence or military operations, but it does mean that we would know how much of our budget is unaccounted for, and how this amount compares to prior periods. For government contractors and subcontractors, this simply means that they would be accountable for what they receive, not just to the government, but to the public. While various levels of accountability and reporting currently exist, the FTS would create transparency and, in fact, could replace some of the existing reporting agencies.

Once the FTS has been established, all entities that are required to use it must report their financials to the FTS with a lag time of no more than 120 days. In other words, no entity reports should be more than 120 days old when submitted. Anything that cannot be reconciled within the 120-day period will be assigned to a discrepancy account and flagged for later resolution. The Freedom Watch group will not only review such discrepancies but will attribute yellow or red flags to FTS reports. Entities will be required to resolve flags within a certain period; otherwise, they will not receive their budgeted money, may be subject to disciplinary actions or, in the case of contractors, will not qualify for future contracts.

Charitable and faith-based entities make significant contributions to society. However, any tax-exempt organization should be considered as in the same category as an organization that receives direct funding from the government. Reporting to the FTS would be a requirement for any organization that receives tax benefits from the government, whether those benefits are in the form of a tax exemption, subsidies, grants, loans, or other aid.

This requirement could be used to the people's advantage if it were expanded to include any corporation whose net taxes fell below 15%, the supposed minimum corporate tax bracket percentage. Imagine the reaction of private and public corporations faced with the dilemma of either publicly revealing their detailed financials to the FTS, showing how they avoided the minimum tax, or paying additional taxes to reach the threshold and avoid such exposure. Don't we really want to know why a corporation pays less tax than the minimum? I do. With such a policy, the public wins either by collecting proper taxes or by learning about the loopholes that corporations use in order to avoid paying taxes. We could use that information to help us close such loopholes.

3

Freedom Watch

★ ★ ★ ★

Our democracy relies on the three independent branches of our government and their accountability to each other, and ultimately to the people. However, this accountability can be exploited by special interest groups as they desire. To correct the corruption in the system, I suggest a group I call Freedom Watch, which would be a nonprofit, volunteer-based organization consisting of many subgroups defined by field of expertise. Its personnel would serve for a limited amount of time and would be selected by their peers. Everyone within a given subgroup would be an expert in that field, and, as such, would provide opinions on issues within their fields. Some subgroups could act as referees by issuing green, yellow, or red flags. The subgroups themselves have no enforcement powers, but their opinions or flags would be used to publicly manage issues.

For example, the accounting subgroup would be responsible for the Financial Transparency Service discussed in the previous chapter. In this subgroup, members would have to be accountants, CPAs, financiers, or economists, or have other expertise in related fields. The accounting subgroup would have the authority to issue flags. Similarly, in the science subgroup various scientists would explore a wide range of issues such as global warming or stem cell research and state their opinions. Yet another example would be the medical subgroup: physicians would address issues such as abortion, the need for specific vaccinations, or the effects of illicit or prescription drugs. Each subgroup would manage an issue independently, rendering opinions on public matters. Some of these subgroups may already exist in various forms and can be reorganized into the Freedom Watch group, which would be recognized by the public as independent and unbiased subject-matter experts.

Subgroups could also include a faith-based group and a media watch group. The faith-based group would consist of people from various faiths who would monitor issues important to their followers. The members of this group might include ministers, priests, rabbis, and imams, working together to create a common ground and to apply their faith traditions to improve society. The media watch group would be tasked with monitoring various media outlets and issuing opinions on their performance with regard to relevant and unbiased reporting.

As with many other suggestions in this book, Freedom Watch should have a website to allow the general public to easily access information on various matters, as well as unresolved flags when the subgroup acts as a referee, as the accounting subgroup would for the FTS. Additionally, anyone who runs for office would be asked to state his or her opinion on every Freedom Watch issue, in the form of yes, no, or pass. This would give us a clear understanding of the candidates' positions on various issues that are important to our society, not just those that are hot at the time of election.

With the creation of the FTS and Freedom Watch, new nonprofit and for-profit organizations would most likely be created to take advantage of the available information. These organizations, in turn, would provide new services leading to further transparencies and efficiencies.

4

The Independent Reporting Organization

★ ★ ★ ★

We take our freedom of speech very seriously—sometimes to the extent of protecting it even when its abuse harms us. As I am writing this book, a new video game, which I do not want to promote by mentioning its name, has been released in which players get to kill Washington, DC, police in full badge and uniform. The game makers use their First Amendment rights to get away with promoting this violence. As much as we may hate what this game company is doing, we tolerate it to protect our freedom of speech.

The First Amendment also guarantees the freedom of the press, so that people can express themselves without interference from the government. Thus our Constitution grants individuals and organizations the right to express themselves freely without the threat or fear of being prosecuted. However, nowhere in the Constitution is anyone required to tell us the truth or deliver unbiased news.

Currently CNN and HLN provide the latest news in a short, precise format to over 99 million American homes.* These news broadcasters are owned by Time Warner, a media conglomerate with a market capitalization of over $69 billion. ABC, NBC, CBS, and FOX provide network news as well as cable news. ABC is owned by the Walt Disney Company, with a market capitalization of over $150 billion. NBC is owned by Comcast with a market capitalization of over $130 billion. CBS is privately held with assets totaling over $26 billion as of the end of 2011.* Fox as well as the *Wall Street Journal* are owned by 21st Century Fox, with a market value of over $70 billion, and News Corp, with a market cap of over $9 billion. Rupert Murdoch is the chairman of both 21st Century Fox and News Corp. Yahoo's market capitalization is over $36 billion. Among other major providers of news are *USA Today*, the *Washington Post*, and the *New York Times. USA Today* is part of Gannett with a cap of over $7 billion. The *Washington Post* is owned by Jeff Bezos, whose net worth is around $30 billion. The *New York Times*'s market cap is about $2 billion, which is the smallest cap of all media outlined here. All market capitalization figures used here were derived from Yahoo Finance.*

What all these companies—public or private, reaching us through radio, television, Internet, or print—have in common is the fact that they are all multi-billion-dollar corporations operating for profit. While there's nothing wrong with operating for profit, there are no guarantees that the drive to generate profit does not influence what's being reported and, more importantly, how it's being reported.

This is not to say that there are no unbiased reporting organizations, but they might as well be on the list of endangered species. We know that we make decisions based on the information we receive, from what to eat to which candidate to vote for. Yet we make no attempt to ensure that we receive timely and accurate information without any lens or filter. I believe that our need to know the facts and the truth surrounding an issue is much greater and more important than anything else, including the need to state our own views. Our opinions are only as valid as the information we have received. If we are told that a dictator has WMDs, then we would, naturally, want to deal with this problem, and many of us would be willing to give our lives to ensure that he would not use them. In short, we can make the right decisions if we are given the right information; thus we must ensure that we receive the most accurate, up-to-date, and unbiased information.

There is nothing new here. In 1967, the United States Congress created the Corporation for Public Broadcasting (CPB), which today operates PBS and NPR.* Among its other objectives, this act of the Congress was intended:

> To encourage the growth and development of public radio and television broadcasting, including the use of such media for instructional, educational, and cultural purposes.

> To encourage public telecommunications services

which will be responsive to the interests of people both in particular localities and throughout the United States.

The act also ensured bipartisan oversight. Although the president appoints the CPB's nine governing board members for their six-year terms with the consent of the Senate, no more than five members may be from the same political party. In addition, "No political test or qualification shall be used in selecting, appointing, promoting, or taking other personnel actions with respect to officers, agents, and employees of the Corporation."

What is missing from this act is independent investigative reporting. There are great unbiased reporters, who have dedicated their lives to their profession. However, investigative reporting requires resources and would not be possible without an independent organization and the necessary budget. While PBS and NPR provide reporting, I suggest that their budget be greatly expanded and their oversight be passed to the Freedom Watch group, which was discussed in the previous chapter. I reason that the Internet, as long as net neutrality is maintained, provides a simple platform for communication, thus reducing our reliance on radio and television. However, with the ever-increasing threats to our freedom, the need for investigative and unbiased reporting is greater than ever. This requires a much larger budget and total independence from the government and private corporations.

I would suggest that the budget for the Independent Reporting Organization (IRO) be pegged to the defense budget. The defense budget is always protected by government contractors and their lobbyists, whereas no influential entity would defend the budget for the IRO. Furthermore, the higher the defense budget, the greater the need for transparency and investigative reporting. Therefore, tying the IRO budget to the defense budget seems like a perfect solution.

Setting the IRO's budget at 0.1% of the defense budget would be a suitable proportion. In 2012, the defense budget was $672.9 billion, which would have made the budget for the IRO $672.9 million. To put this figure in perspective, NPR revenues in 2011 were about $177 million from all sources.* Whatever we can afford spending in military might to defend ourselves from foreign threats, we can spend one thousandth of that amount to protect our freedom through unbiased, independent reporting.

With the availability of the Internet, the CPB should change its focus to independent reporting. NPR can continue using corporate sponsorship as part of its revenue, but must remain diligent not to allow sponsorships to affect its reporting.

While nothing may guarantee unbiased reporting, NPR's new budget and independent oversight by the Freedom Watch group will go a long way. Having a strong independent outlet encourages and ensures that other unbiased reporting agencies remain and thrive. Without accurate information, we are neither wise nor effective. Information can be our greatest ally or our archenemy. With it, we can accomplish wonders, but without it, we are slaves to our own democracy. The IRO's mission would be to provide us with relevant, timely, and unbiased information.

5

The First Amendment

★ ★ ★ ★

It is ironic that the very First Amendment, intended to protect us, is used against us every day. It is used to insult our beliefs. It is used to sell us alcohol, lottery tickets, and prescription drugs. It is used to degrade our morality. And it is used to promote violence in our children.

The issue is that we view our First Amendment rights as absolute and unconditional, whereas, as discussed earlier, nothing is absolute. We need to understand that the purpose of the First Amendment, and every law, is to protect the people. Corporations, on the other hand, should enjoy their freedom of speech as long as such freedom is not being used against the people and does not hurt the people. A company promoting a violent game against police officers must not be protected under the First Amendment's guaranteed freedom of speech. We need to protect people, not companies. Each year, corporations spend billions on advertising, because ads work. Therefore, to promote a healthy society we need to ensure that we are not subject to the type of advertisements that destroy our society.

The best example of advertising at work is smoking. Cigarette ads were commonplace just a few decades ago. Now there are barely any ads for cigarettes, and far fewer smokers. The decline in smoking should be partly credited to Hollywood, which we will talk about later.

The law should not allow advertisements for products or services that are harmful or designed to influence us in a negative way. Here are some other examples.

Alcohol: We cannot show a beautiful girl in someone's arms while drinking and having a blast, then conclude the ad with a "drink responsibly" message, and expect that people will drink responsibly. We know the ad is not designed to encourage anyone to drink responsibly, and some will not do so. If we intended for people to drink responsibly, we'd stop advertising alcohol or show a fatal car crash as the result of drunk driving. Then people would drink responsibly.

Illegal drugs and prostitution: As will be discussed in later chapters, legalizing some of our temptations would enable the redirection of resources to more important areas and remove methods of controlling minorities. It is easy to predict that if we legalize illicit drugs or prostitution, they will be promoted through advertising. Once we legalize either one of them, we should also ban any advertisement promoting them. It is relatively easy to teach our children that legal does not mean ethical, but our job is much harder when these vices are publicly promoted.

Gambling and the lottery: Although the lottery is commonplace, it is still gambling, and while it should remain legal, it should not be glorified by advertisements.

Prescription drugs: Ads should not tell me to ask my doctor for a medication. If my doctor believes that I need a certain medicine, he or she will prescribe it. Advertising prescription drugs is just legally pushing drugs. Pharmaceutical companies should stop advertising drugs that require a prescription, and if they still want to promote them, they can use the money not spent on advertising to instead create a fund for those who cannot afford their medications. Additionally, pharmaceutical companies spent $4 billion between 2009 and 2014 to promote their products to healthcare providers.* If you visit this site, you can find out if your doctor has received money from a pharmaceutical company: https://projects.propublica.org/docdollars/.* I also view this spending as improper conduct to say the least, but I am not suggesting a ban on it as I believe that pharmaceutical companies would just find a way around it.

Weapons manufacturers and defense contractors: As civilians, we are neither qualified to evaluate what is necessary and suitable for our nation's defense nor are we customers for defense contractors' products. It is bad enough that these manufacturers and contractors lobby our representatives to sell their products and services, but it is even worse when they buy media time to win our votes. It is wrong for the media to tell us what ship, plane, missile, or service our military should buy.

6

Hollywood and the Gaming Industry

★ ★ ★ ★

Hollywood and the video game industry can play a positive or negative role in our lives and the lives of our children. In the television series *Mad Men*, which is about an ad agency in the sixties, executives are shown smoking when and where they want to. At the time, smoking was a sign of power and privilege. In fact, it would be difficult to find an old movie that portrayed smoking negatively. In contrast, in modern Hollywood, lighting a cigarette is mostly reserved for those in some kind of stress or in poverty. Hollywood plays a big role in our children's lives, and it is easy to see a correlation between Hollywood's portrayal of smoking and what our teens do. The change in smoking reflects how Hollywood can be a positive influence. In contrast, the movie and gaming industries constantly promote gore and violence and demean the value of life.

Both gaming and movie industries already have ratings in place. The ratings for games are "C" for early childhood, "E" (everyone), "E10+" (Everyone 10+), "T" (Teen, 13 and up), "M" (Mature, 17 and up), and "A" (Adult Only, 18 and up). The ratings for movies are "G" (General Audience), "PG" (Parental Guidance), "PG-13" (13 and up), "R" (Restricted), and "NC-17" (no one under 17 is admitted). You can read more about these ratings at http://www.esrb.org for games and http://www.mpaa.org for movies.

Language, nudity, sex, and violence affect the ratings. I believe that the current rating is not sufficient for material of extreme violent nature and a separate rating should be assigned to warn both children and parents. To make my point, I would suggest reading the description of the violent scenes in *Kingsman: The Secret Service*, which has an "R" rating. Let me warn you that even the description may be disturbing to you.*

Scenes that desensitize the audience to real or animated violence of extreme nature, regardless of their duration, should be classified with a "V" rating. A "V" rated movie would be treated the same as an "R" rated one, but "V" rating clearly indicates the extremely violent nature of the movie. It is interesting that we are much quicker to warn consumers of nudity and sex than violence, since none of us would be alive if our parents had not had sex, yet violence deprives us and our loved ones from life, happiness, and peace.

7

Requiring ID for Voting

★ ★ ★ ★

Requiring an ID to vote does not violate our freedom. Our freedom is protected when we can trust an election, and an election can be trusted only if we can verify the identity of the voter, ensure that the voter is freely exercising the right of voting, and be confident that the voter will only cast one vote. To do so, a photo ID must be required for voting. Any government-issued photo ID, such as a driver's license, passport, or military card, should be acceptable. All states should also provide free voter IDs if the voter has no photo ID or desires to have a voter ID.

8

Mr. President and His Birth Certificate

★ ★ ★ ★

To become the United States president, according to the Constitution, one must be a natural-born citizen of the United States, thirty-five years of age or older, and a resident for fourteen years.*

I believe that the requirements should be more stringent. When the Constitution was written, it took six to twelve weeks to make the transatlantic journey, which was a life-threatening endeavor. In addition, immigration was primarily cross-continent. Now, of course, it takes less than a day to get here from even the most distant places on earth, and there is no danger when it's done legally. In addition, half of US immigrants are from other countries in the Americas.*

Today, it's quite possible that a presidential candidate could be born in the US, grow up in his parents' native country, and return to the US for higher education and in order to be eligible by the age of thirty-five. While this is fine for other positions, it is a very low standard to qualify for the most powerful position in the US—the president of the United States, who holds the key to a nuclear arsenal and whose Executive Order can triumph in Congress.

We need to make this requirement tougher. A candidate for the US presidency must be a third-generation American. Additionally, a candidate's parents and grandparents must be natural-born American citizens, unless they were born abroad while their family members were on active duty for the US armed forces, in the State Department, or serving the country in a similar manner.

When we elect a president only to debate where he was born, no matter how farfetched the speculation is, we weaken the presidency. Additional requirements for presidential candidacy ensure the American way of life, which is what attracts immigrants to America in the first place.

9

Simple Majority Election

★ ★ ★ ★

S ome things are complex in nature, such as sending a man to the moon, while some are supposed to be simple. Elections are supposed to be simple. In a presidential election, if Al Gore gets more votes than George W. Bush, Al Gore should win the election! But that is not how it works.

We elect our president through the Electoral College process, which functions as follows: There are 538 electors, one for each member of Congress and three for the District of Columbia.* A majority of 270 electoral votes is required to elect a president. When we vote for a candidate, in reality, we vote for the candidate's electors. In most states, electors are not required to vote according to the popular votes or vote at all, but historically, over 99% voted as pledged.* With the exception of Maine and Nebraska, all states use a "winner-take-all" system. For example, Virginia, where I live, has thirteen electors. If a candidate gets 51% of the votes in Virginia, he or she would not get 51% of the electoral votes, or in this case, seven votes. Rather, the candidate would get all thirteen of Virginia's votes.

We can sum up the problems with the Electoral College by reviewing the results of the 2000 election, in which Al Gore received 540,520 more votes than George W. Bush, but Bush won the election with 271 electoral votes to Gore's 266. Simply put, we voted for Gore by a margin of over half a million votes, but Bush became the president. In another country, this would be considered fraud! For those of you who have done the math and realized that the electoral vote was short by one—this was because one elector did not vote. That is right, one elector did not vote.

If the point of democracy is that people elect their president, then the 2000 presidential election clearly showed that it is not so and exemplified the flaws of the Electoral College process.

According to Marc Schulman, one purpose of the Electoral College was, in fact, to reserve the ability to override the popular vote.

> Hamilton and the other founders did not trust the population to make the right choice . . . They believed that with the Electoral College no one would be able to manipulate the citizenry.*

Another goal was to satisfy the smaller states. Since the number of electors is linked to the number of congressmen, and because each state has two senators regardless of its population, the individual votes in smaller states carry more weight than in larger states. According to FairVote.org, "each individual vote in Wyoming counts nearly four times as much in the Electoral College as each individual vote in Texas."* Refer to this link to find out how much your vote counts: http://www.fairvote.org/assets/Uploads/npv/2008voters-perelector.pdf. *

Changing the Electoral College system to popular vote requires an amendment to the Constitution, which requires that three-fourths of the states agree to this amendment. In thirty-three states, individual votes carry more weight and in seventeen states, they carry less weight. The states whose votes carry more weight may not agree to depart from the Electoral College system. This simply means that it may be unlikely to get three-fourths of states to agree to such a change.

Nevertheless, democracy suffers due to the Electoral College process. Democrats are not represented in Republican states and Republicans are not represented in Democratic states. In other words, if you vote Democrat in a majority Republican state, your vote is useless. That is undemocratic, and as a nation proud of its democracy, we need to change our election system.

If "all men are created equal," then everyone's vote should count equally. The Electoral College system is outdated and flawed; yet it seems unlikely that we will ever get rid of it. So what is the solution? Take a moment to think about this.

The National Popular Vote Bill offers a genius yet simple solution and is already on its way to solving this monumental issue.* According to National Popular Vote website:

Under the National Popular Vote bill, all of the state's electoral votes would be awarded to the presidential candidate who receives the most popular votes in all 50 states and the District of Columbia. The bill would take effect only when enacted, in identical form, by states possessing a majority of the electoral votes — that is, enough electoral votes to elect a President (270 of 538).

The bill needs 270 electoral votes to get enacted. It already has 165 electoral votes from eleven jurisdictions.

It is critical for our nation to address this issue, so please visit this site: **www.nationalpopularvote.com**, enter your zip code, and with a few clicks you can play a role in making a change.* Making a change for the better is what YFOG is all about.

10

Presidential Elections – *American Idol* Style

★ ★ ★ ★

When a presidential campaign requires billions of dollars, democracy suffers. On May 23, 2012, 132 million votes were cast for the final two contestants, Phillip Phillips and Jessica Sanchez, by the viewers of the eleventh season of *American Idol*.* The highest number of votes ever cast in a presidential election, 129 million, was in 2008.* Here is the major difference between *American Idol* and the presidential election: During the idol contest, we discovered the backgrounds and qualities of each finalist, in addition to how well they can sing and perform. Within a few months, we saw them evolve into artists and performers. We learned about their habits, personalities, and potential. Before the 2008 presidential election, we did not know much about Senator Obama. But unlike in *American Idol*, we knew Senator McCain well at the start of the campaign. At the time, we badly needed change, so Senator Obama's campaign managers made this the cornerstone of his campaign. Senator McCain could not have promised change, even if he wanted to. He had spent too much time in public service, and his opinions were too clear for him to run a campaign on such a theme. The rest is history. Of course, change was just a campaign slogan, but we still need it. We need to change our election system.

There is another major difference between *American Idol* and the presidential election. In *American Idol*, two unfamiliar candidates reached the finals through their own means, and one won. In the 2008 presidential election, more than $2.6 billion was spent, and still one candidate won. We should have an idea of what a billion is by now. Are we to believe that $2.6 billion was spent to ensure that the most suitable presidential candidate would win? Do we believe that a free election requires a $2.6 billion budget?* In 2012, the average campaign budget for winning US House and Senate candidates was $1.6 million and $10.3 million, respectively.* No wonder we the people are not represented.

We need to create an *American Idol*–style presidential election. The show could be produced by Hollywood, and the search for candidates would start two or three years prior to the election. Judges would be members of the Freedom Watch group, and rather than three or four judges, there would be dozens. The panel of judges could include experts in foreign relations, military, science, economics, and other fields; it could consist of university professors, journalists, and former politicians, among others. For each week of the first year, the show would take place in a different state. These weekly shows would be specifically designed for the audience to learn about the candidates and their positions on issues raised by the Freedom Watch group. The elimination process would then start in the second year. Throughout the show, people's votes would be tallied as a measure of the candidates' and the show's popularity. The elimination process would take place through the judges' votes. The show would team up the two finalists as candidates for president and vice president in the upcoming election. The nominees for president and vice president would then be promoted by the show, which should be captivating enough to generate its own revenue. While Hollywood should have no problem keeping the show engaging, additional funding may be raised through campaign fundraising. This campaign fundraising could be a form of voting. People could vote by donating, which would be subject to campaign financing rules.

The *American Idol*–style presidential election would not replace traditional elections or require any changes in the current election laws. When the elections roll around, the American Idol finalists would run as an independent candidate and receive votes as any presidential candidate does. If carried out correctly, the show's success would change our elections and reduce our reliance on the Democratic and Republican parties. After all, we do not elect a political party to be president. We elect an individual, whom we believe in and trust! The absence of party affiliation further allows candidates to serve the people and not the interests or agenda of any party. The lack of affiliation also allows the candidate to work with various parties freely, without any chance of gridlock. If the show proves to work for the presidential election, it could be replicated for other political races.

11

Politicians

★ ★ ★ ★

So it takes millions or billions of dollars to become a representative, a senator, or a president. *American Idol–*style elections could level the playing field and allow ordinary citizens to represent us, without our politicians relying on lobbyists' funding. This, however, does not address greedy politicians, who may see the office as a get-rich-quick scheme. For some candidates, the trend is to use the rich to fund their campaign, and then to return the favor through legislation once they are elected. After they leave office, they secure advisory positions, join a board of directors, or become lobbyists to get compensation for their work in office and to continue pulling strings with their colleagues. The system works for politicians, but not for the people.

I believe that for every bad seed, there are at least ten good ones—ten people who, given the opportunity, would serve their country with honor and, when done, go back to living their lives. This is how it should be; serving the country is a privilege and an honor, not a get-rich-quick scheme. How can greed be taken out of the equation? Perhaps the introduction of a lifetime income cap would be the answer. Another answer may be to make it illegal for politicians to work as lobbyists or for government contractors after they serve their term. Additionally, we can make it illegal for government contractors to commission former politicians. But these solutions would be too problematic and too punitive for those who serve their offices with honor. If some of the other solutions offered in this book are implemented, this may not be as big an issue any longer. Nevertheless, I do not have a good solution for political greed.

12

A Contract with the People

★ ★ ★ ★

How often does a candidate run a campaign on the promise of addressing or resolving an issue, only to get our votes and not deliver on the promise? A campaign promise should be treated as a contract with the people. As with any contract, the candidate's failure to take reasonable steps toward fulfilling his or her promise should be considered a breach of contract.

I am not suggesting that this breach be criminalized, but, at the very least, the candidate guilty of the breach should be disqualified from running for reelection. If a candidate does not fulfill his or her promise while in office, at a minimum it means that he or she was unable to make a good assessment of what it would take to fulfill the promise. At worst, he or she did not intend to fulfill that promise in the first place. Either

way, unfulfilled campaign promises are not signs of a qualified candidate.

13

Pit Stop 1

★ ★ ★ ★

To control the flow of money, we created financial transparency, and we subjected to it our biggest spenders, the government and government contractors, as well as nonprofit organizations. We know that our government is inefficient, but we also know that the private sector is for profit and not for the people, so we expanded the role of nonprofit organizations to keep our government on track.

We created a volunteer organization, Freedom Watch, which consists of individuals in specialized subgroups, who have high levels of expertise within their fields. In this way, we have a trusted source of expertise on various issues and an independent oversight to separate noise from what matters and to keep us focused on what's important.

We created the Independent Reporting Organization (IRO) to ensure that we receive the right information, and we granted its oversight to the Freedom Watch group. With this unbiased reporting in place, we also ensured that we are not manipulated through advertisements. We limited ads on alcohol, tobacco, drugs (prescription or illicit), and gambling, as well as ads by government contactors designed to sway our vote in their favor. We raised Hollywood's standards and those of the gaming industry so that they stop promoting gore and violence to our families and children.

We then turned our attention to politicians. First, we made a government-issued photo ID a requirement to vote in order to remove any ambiguity from the process. Second, we ensured that whoever becomes the president is at least a third-generation American. Third, we ensured that our votes count by adopting a popular vote election through the National Popular Vote. Fourth, with *American Idol*–style elections, we made it possible for candidates to run for office without the need for billion-dollar campaigns. Fifth, we asked candidates to debate the issues raised by the Freedom Watch group, not just the politically charged ones. Sixth, we determined that each candidate's campaign promises would constitute a contract with their constituents and that we would ban the candidate from running again if the contract were breached. With these rules in place, we ensured that any patriot can run for any office exclusively to serve the people.

14

Legal Age

★ ★ ★ ★

The age at which one crosses from being a child to being an adult is known as the age of majority, as opposed to being a minor. This age has been raised in the last two centuries.* In earlier times, the age was related to puberty, and as such was around nine and thirteen for girls and boys respectively. At that time, one's age may not have been clear in the first place since no official birth records were maintained. The age of majority, as we recognize it today, has been established to differentiate children from adults, but at some point not even the concept of childhood existed. As people grew older, they were recognized for their abilities, mostly based on their physical appearance and mental maturity, without crossing a distinct line from childhood to adulthood, as we do today.

While universally a line between childhood and adulthood exists, its meaning and the age at which this line is crossed still vary greatly around the world. In the US, there is not a single line that one crosses, but various lines for various purposes. The ones often mistaken are the age of majority and the age of consent, or the age of sexual consent. Other age limits include drinking age, smoking age, and voting age among others. The age of majority is the age at which one takes control of his or her own life as an adult. This age is eighteen in the US, except in Alabama and Nebraska, where it is nineteen, and in Mississippi and Puerto Rico, where the age is twenty-one. The voting age in the US is eighteen.

Regarding the age of sexual consent, a person below this age is considered a victim and above it an offender. This definition is being used here to address the age of consent. In a later chapter, we will talk about the decriminalization of sexual acts when those involved are young and close in age. The age of consent varies greatly and could depend on various factors including the nature of the act, the genders and roles of participants, and whether they are married or not. By federal law it is sixteen, but it ranges from fifteen to eighteen depending on the state.*

The age at which one may get married in the US is eighteen, except in Nebraska, where it is nineteen.* The minimum age to join the US armed forces or become a licensed pilot is seventeen.* The minimum age for consuming alcoholic beverages is twenty-one, and one must be eighteen to buy cigarettes in most states, but nineteen or twenty-one in a few of them. And the list goes on.

So in short, depending where you live, sex is allowed as early as fifteen, driving when one is sixteen, piloting planes or joining the military at seventeen, getting married or having a say in the laws governing us by voting at eighteen, and drinking at twenty-one. There are enough variations and exceptions state by state for a whole book on the subject.

I suggest that the age of majority, the age of marriage, the age of consent, and the age of voting be consolidated into a legal age of sixteen. Simply, one may get married, have sex, run his or her own venture, and have a say in who gets elected when one is sixteen years of age. In my education reform, this is also the age when one will obtain a HS diploma. We can maintain a higher age limit for smoking, drinking, or other matters that may have more severe consequences at a younger age.

Confusing laws with many varieties and exceptions may work greatly for lawyers, but not necessarily for everyone else who needs to obey these laws. I will also address this complexity in the Sunset Clause chapter.

We need to reduce the legal voting age to sixteen to allow society to have a voice at a younger age. Allowing our children to be involved in determining their future can fundamentally change our society. A two-year shift would allow our children to get involved with politics at a younger age.

Besides emotional reasons, there is no legitimate reason for the current legal age. From the brain development perspective, consider this passage from MIT's Young Adult Development Project:

> As a number of researchers have put it, "the rental car companies have it right." The brain isn't fully mature at 16, when we are allowed to drive, or at 18, when we are allowed to vote, or at 21, when we are allowed to drink, but closer to 25, when we are allowed to rent a car.*

But the legal age isn't twenty-five, so brain development is obviously not our criterion. If a sixteen-year-old can drive a car, co-pilot a plane, and have sexual intercourse, he or she is also mature enough and possesses sufficient power of deduction and reasoning to vote, get married, or be considered an adult. We have previously reduced the voting age from twenty-one to eighteen, and it is important to our future to reduce it once again.

15

K–10

★ ★ ★ ★

Our K-12 education system has been failing us for a long time, and most solutions suggest that we increase the length of schooling. In the past, when one received a doctorate degree, he or she was considered a scientist and an expert in any field. Since then, our knowledge has tremendously expanded, requiring us to specialize. Nowadays it would sound ridiculous to expect a surgeon with over twenty years of education to also know how to repair his lawn mower, much less build a cell phone, program a website, or fix a wristwatch! The scope of human knowledge has expanded radically, requiring us to know more in order to excel.

The weight of this expanded learning has not been distributed equally between a high-school diploma and an undergraduate or graduate degree. At the university level, students specialize and learn what is required for specific degrees. While our knowledge expands, students' learning does not; students instead become more specialized as newer fields and related degrees are created. High schools, in contrast, carry a heavier load to prepare their students for this expanded knowledge.

Along with this expansion of knowledge, our expectations for various degrees have also changed. There was a time when reading, writing, and understanding simple mathematics were the only requirements to obtain a white-collar job or become a successful businessman. Later, a high-school diploma became the minimum requirement. Today, everyone is expected to have one, but it's not clear what to expect from the recipient of this diploma.

At the low end of expectations, we assume that someone with a high-school diploma has mastered reading and writing, yet statistically, we know this is not the case.* On the higher end of our expectations, high school should prepare one for college. However, colleges do not expect high-school graduates to possess the necessary knowledge to successfully go through college, and rightfully so. Freshmen at universities and colleges often spend part or all of the year preparing, repeating some of the same courses taken in high school, and often taking new introductory courses to ensure a solid base before declaring a major. What no one expects from a high-school graduate is to know a profession.

The education problem is greatly magnified by the lack of uniformity among the states, within state districts, and even in schools within the same district. The lack of a standard is worsened by racial disparities, which begin during preschool, according to Attorney General Eric Holder. According to the Department of Education:

Black students represent 18% of preschool enroll-
ment but 42% of students suspended once, and 48%
of the students suspended more than once.

Less than half of American Indian and Native-Alaskan
high-school students have access to a full range of
math and science courses in their high school.*

If, after spending thirteen of the most precious years of
one's life in school, one does not have a command of the language, does not know a profession, and is not ready to pursue
a higher degree, then surely a person should at least be ready
to enter society, with a comprehensive understanding of earth-
lings. We should undoubtedly know about our human psy-
che, our bodies, nutrition, and how to keep ourselves healthy.
We should know about our planet, its geography, various
cultures, their languages, and what's important to them. We
should know about people's faiths, their aspirations, the history of mankind, our country, and more. Sadly, a high-school
diploma does not guarantee knowledge of any of this.

Most people spend thirteen years in school not preparing for college, not learning a profession, and not becoming
an informed member of society, yet most high schools offer
everything under the sun, from advanced physics and algebra
to literature, art, music, geography, history, social sciences,
and more. Our high schools offer everything, and a high-
school diploma gets us nothing.

I believe it is time to change our educational system, and
we should start by defining the purpose of a diploma. This

is what I would expect from someone with a high-school diploma:

- Mastery of one or two languages. Knowledge does not matter if we cannot communicate efficiently.
- A clear understanding of human anatomy, its development from womb to grave, its nutritional needs, and the sources of such nutrition. It is also important to understand how our physical being interacts with our environment. To efficiently use a machine, we need to understand how it works, and our body is one machine that we cannot live without.
- Knowledge of peoples of the world, their countries, languages, faiths, economies, and what's distinctive about them. We are a social species, so we must know about others in order to effectively interact with them.
- Knowledge of the history of earth, mankind, and the United States.
- Knowledge of basic sciences and the scientific principles governing our universe. To understand our world, we need to learn the laws that govern it.
- The required skills to use the communication tools available to us. We increasingly rely on technology to succeed; we must know how to use it.
- An awareness of one's passion and talents. We need to know what we want to do after high school.

With these objectives in mind, K–12 should be reduced to K–10, so that our children would graduate from high school by age 16. Then they should attend either a four-year undergraduate program or a three-year vocational school that would involve a paid internship during the last year. In other words, every student who does not plan to get a master's or doctorate degree must know a trade or have a profession. The three-year vocational schools should offer curricula to accommodate a wide range of professions, such as administrative assistant, bookkeeper, electrician, mechanic, musician, plumber, professional driver, programmer, repairman, roofer, and so on.

This will change how we look at education; rather than a theoretical exercise, it will be a practical one. Our children will be able to attend graduate school by the time they are nineteen, or they will have already worked in their profession as interns for a year. This would radically lower the cost of education and increase our productivity, but more importantly, it places possessing a skill, such as plumbing or roofing, on the same level as having a bachelor's degree—as it should be. We will talk about vocational schools in another chapter.

Fifteen-year-old students from the US ranked thirty-sixth in the world in math, reading, and science in 2012. The Chinese ranked first.* We need to recognize the importance of education and its purpose at each stage. We then must redistribute our resources to create a minimum standard so that every child has access to a preschool and the same level of education in K-10 regardless of the state, district, or school. Addressing the disparity in our K–10 education system has much broader effects on our freedom, equality, and productivity. The reduction of K–12 to K–10 requires changes in the curriculum, which we will discuss in a different chapter.

16

English or Spanish

★ ★ ★ ★

nglish or Spanish? Our current reality begs the question: Why not both? Why don't many US citizens speak a second language, and why shouldn't immigrants be required to speak English fluently? First, the bar for the English requirement for residency and citizenship must be raised. To qualify, applicants must be able to speak conversational English and to read and write in English. It is difficult to believe the argument that the country is good enough to be adopted as a home, but not good enough to prompt learning its official language. Speaking English does not mean understanding and assimilating to American culture, but not speaking English guarantees the lack of such understanding or assimilation.

There are enough Spanish speakers in the United States to put Americans who do not speak Spanish at a disadvantage.* Considering our 450 million Spanish-speaking neighbors to the south, speaking Spanish will also give Americans the advantage of more fully understanding our neighbors and expanding commerce with them.

Our neighbor to the north, Canada, has English and French as its official languages. I do not believe that the US should adopt Spanish as an official language, but rather require learning Spanish as a second language. While many countries either have two or more official languages or offer a second language in their education system, Luxembourg is a good example of what I am suggesting. It not only has three official languages — French, German, and Luxembourgish — it also ensures that everyone learns all three languages as their primary languages. Students learn English or other languages additionally.

All Americans, regardless of their country of origin, must have a strong command of the English language, and Spanish should be required as a second language. By the time our children leave elementary school, they should be able to speak both English and Spanish fluently.

17

National Curriculum

★ ★ ★ ★

Our K–12 school curricula vary greatly from one district to another, and generally they do not produce the desired result. In the chapter K–10, we discussed the set of objectives that our schools should achieve as well as the need to reduce K–12 to K–10 in order to meet these objectives. We will also discuss the addition of a three-year vocational bachelor's degree program in the next chapter.

A change in curricula is necessary to ensure that the objectives of K–10 are met, but it is important to point out that if we emphasize a subject less, the subject is not unimportant. It simply means that the subject does not play a vital role in meeting our objectives. In short, the curricula should be aligned with what we are looking for in our high-school graduates.

In my opinion, K-10 education should allow us to discover our passion and prepare us for higher education. Additionally, it should turn us into informed members of society. Higher education should train us for our passions, our talents, and our professions.

To accommodate K–10 as well as changes in the curricula, it is imperative that we have capable educators and an adequate infrastructure. Fortunately, we enjoy a great pool of skilled teachers, who are very passionate and dedicated. We also have a great infrastructure, with buildings, equipment, and transportation that can support these changes.

To start with, K–10 education would mean either kindergarten, a six-year elementary school and four-year high school, or kindergarten, a five-year elementary and five-year high school, eliminating middle school in both cases.

To ensure that our educational system is effective and affordable, but more importantly, that it promotes equality, we need to standardize the curricula and require the same courses throughout all our public schools, hence the national curriculum. These courses will be taught as they are now, but both teachers and students would take standardized tests each quarter. The students' results would determine their grades, and teachers' scores would be a factor in their rankings.

The current electives offered throughout our schools would be replaced by online courses. These online courses would be available to all schools. A knowledge base would be created and Educational Virtual Attendants (EVA) would respond to students' questions, much as Siri, a voice-enabled personal assistant offered on some Apple devices, does today.* Similar to Siri, EVA will take advantage of a knowledge base, web service, and natural language user interface to interact with students. All components to create EVA already exist, and EVA can be offered through private or nonprofit companies. EVA would not only reduce the cost of education but could also play a major role in the standardization of it.

Depending on school size, two or more local facilitators would ensure that these online classes are taken and that students' questions are answered. This would replace the many teachers needed for electives with a general facilitator whose expertise is in education, not in a particular subject. The replaced teachers can fill positions at vocational schools, as will be discussed later, in the chapter on three-year vocational degrees. The money saved can be spent on improving infrastructures.

A set of standards known as Common Core State Standards have been adopted by forty-three states, the District of Columbia, and four territories.* The Common Core is defined as

> The knowledge and skills students should gain throughout their K–12 education in order to graduate high school prepared to succeed in entry-level careers, introductory academic college courses, and workforce training programs.

Common Core is limited to English language arts/ literacy and math. While what I am suggesting may seem like a greatly expanded Common Core, the not-so-obvious differences are critical. I believe that a national curriculum should serve the objectives set for a high-school diploma. However, these objectives distinguish what I am suggesting from the Common Core. While I offer a sample curriculum here, ultimately it should be the Freedom Watch group, rather than a private entity, who should devise the national curriculum. When it does, it is also important to leave room for each state to add what's important to the state.

I offer the following changes to support these objectives for K–10:

- To master one or two languages.
  - ♦ Spanish should be taught alongside English from first grade through sixth grade, with refresher courses from grades 7 through 10. English and literature should be taught from first through tenth grade.
- To have a clear understanding of human anatomy, its development from womb to grave, its nutritional needs and the sources of such nutrition, and its interaction with the environment.
  - ♦ Add a course called Human Biology to the end of elementary school. This course would be composed of human anatomy, nutrition, and health and lifestyle information. The course would not be a politically correct guide to getting slim fast, but a fact-based course to teach about our body, its organs, and their functions, as well as our nutritional needs. It would also teach the natural sources of such nutrition, the side effects of their absence, and dietary guidance for a healthy life. The course would offer an understanding of diet, obesity, exercise, and the environmental factors that cause common health issues such as diabetes.

- To have an understanding of people and their countries, languages, economic systems, their faiths, and what is important to them.

  ♦ Add a geography course to the elementary-school curriculum. This course should start in first grade and continue through third grade. A refresher course should be required later. The recommended geography course is a compilation of relatively simple and relevant facts such as the location of countries, their capitals, their languages, population, overall geography, main body of water or topology, currency, etc. Our students should be able to identify every country on the map, name its capital and its language or languages, and know its approximate population, its main faith, its current system of government, its currency, its main exports, its natural resources, and its geographical landmarks. We are talking about knowing only a handful of facts about fewer than 200 countries. In addition to that, they should know the continents, oceans, seas, and any other major landmarks such as the Amazon, the Nile, the Andes, etc. Last but not least, they ought to know about the United States, be able to name and identify each territory, state, and its capital on the map, and know its natural resources and population, as well as any other important facts. World geography (placement of countries and major landmarks) would be taught in first grade, followed by facts (population, languages, etc.) about the countries in second grade, followed by more detailed facts about the US in third grade. To ensure that every child has learned this subject, a refresher course would be offered each year throughout high school.

♦ The other course added to K–10 to cover our objectives, to be taught in similar fashion to geography, would be religion. The point of this course is not to convert anyone, but to ensure that our students understand what others believe. Many actions taken by individuals, corporations, or governments are driven by their beliefs, and understanding such drivers is critical to our individual successes and to living in harmony. This course would be based on a textbook developed specifically for this purpose, which would include a single page of facts about each established faith. The book itself should be limited to twenty pages. The number of followers of a faith may be used to define an "established faith" or what faiths should be studied. This would reduce the chances of this course becoming another political issue. The top twenty faiths, identified by their number of followers, will make it into the textbook. The fact sheet on each faith will be written by an authority on the subject. The textbook would not allow comparisons, propaganda, or the diminishing or deprecation of any faith. Teachers would be trained and guided to maintain neutrality as this course is not meant to convert or influence students, but to promote our understanding of each other.

Any child who grows up knowing these simple facts about our world and its population would have a much broader view of the world.

- To better understand our history, including the history of earth, mankind, and our country.
    - ◆ Here I believe that we need an overhaul of how we teach history. My suggestion is that history courses be reduced in length and breadth. Experts in history should compile a list of what they believe is critical for every American to know. This list would most likely include a brief history of the universe, followed by a brief history of mankind through different periods, the history of different dynasties, the major wars, and finally, American history.
    - ◆ The department of education and historians should then work with Hollywood to produce a series of movies to cover all the material to be learned (think of the movie *Troy* or *The Ten Commandments*). Each major historical event would be covered in a movie. These movies could be produced and screened for profit initially, and then become public domain in the US. Each movie could accompany a short textbook covering names, places, events, and major dates such as when the US gained its independence and when the world wars started and ended. The textbook would be available online and the same information would appear on screen as subtitles. For example, when Julius Caesar is on the screen, his

name would be displayed. The movie itself not only covers what happened but addresses the whys and their consequences.

The movies, text, and tests would be standardized and available to anyone at any time online, once they enter the public domain. Parents may introduce their children to the material when they think it is appropriate; otherwise, students would learn the material in school. Tests on history, geography, and religion would be taken in every year of high school. These tests would be pass-fail, although at least three passes in four years would be required for a diploma. Students should be required to score 75% or better to pass the tests.

The fact that the materials are freely available and taught at a younger age, and that history is presented as a movie, will allow our students to remember and carry that knowledge with them throughout their lives.

- To understand basic sciences and the laws governing our universe.
  - ♦ These courses include basic math, algebra, geometry, physics, chemistry, biology, data analysis, and economics. All science courses are taught at a basic level, which would be part of the standard curriculum and required for all students. The basic science courses should be spread out over the ten-year period. Any advanced science courses would be optional and offered online.
- To understand and acquire skills to use the communication tools available to us.

♦ Add a course to teach students the basics of personal computing and the principles of information technology, as well as the latest tools available for communication and research.
- To discover our passions and our natural skills.
  ♦ The discovery of one's passions takes place through the entire K–10 schooling process. A required course about undergraduate degrees would familiarize students with their options, required skills, typical financial compensation, and the pros and cons of each field.

I have suggested that a few subjects, such as geography, history, and religion, be taught in a condensed format and at an earlier age. Since I believe that everyone should know the material covered in these subjects, I am suggesting that students take refresher courses in high school. A refresher course will last an hour a week for a quarter of the year or the entire year, depending on the subject.

Following is a sample of the national curriculum for K–10 education:

- English – grades K through 10
- Spanish – grades 1 through 5 with refresher courses in grades 6 through 10
- Geography – grades 1 through 5 with refresher courses in grades 6 through 10
- Basic Science – grades 1 through 5
- History – grades 7 and/or 8 with refresher courses in grade 8 or 9

- Human Biology – grades 4 and 5 with refresher courses in grade 6 or 7
- Religion – grade 6 with refresher course in grade 10
- Information Technology – grades 1 through 10
- Higher Education Orientation – grade 9
- Basic Chemistry – grade 7
- Basic Physics – grade 8
- Basic Mathematics – grades K through 6
- Algebra – grades 7 and 9
- Geometry – grade 8
- Data Analysis – grade 10
- Economics and Personal Finance – grades 7 and 8
- Civics – grade 8
- Physical Education – grades 1 through 5
- Music and Art – grades 1 through 5
- State-sponsored course – grade is determined by each state

Elective Courses: two courses from the subjects listed below in grades 7 through 10:

- Foreign Languages (other than Spanish)
- Music
- Arts
- Advanced Science

I remind you that the curriculum suggested here is a sample and the final curriculum should be devised by the Freedom Watch group.

18

Three-Year Vocational Degree

★ ★ ★ ★

It is clear that a high-school diploma is no longer sufficient to meet the demands of modern society, even when the diploma accomplishes its goals. The needs of our society increasingly rely on skilled jobs and specialized knowledge and training. The K–12 system or K–10 system, as I have suggested in prior chapters, is not designed to provide students with any specialized training, but only with general knowledge. Because of the vast amount of information now available, the K–10 system, armed with a national curriculum, will ensure that everyone meets the standard requirements to be an informed member of society when he or she receives a high-school diploma. Then colleges (I do not differentiate colleges from universities) will provide students with a specific set of knowledge or skills.

There are currently high schools that offer vocational

programs. Some schools in Massachusetts, for example, offer a range of vocational skills from agriculture to transportation. However, these schools are exceptions rather than the norm and highlight the inconsistency in our national education system. Most schools do not offer any vocational program, and a typical high-school graduate is not prepared to excel at any job and must obtain a college degree or higher education. That is why possessing a bachelor's degree should be the norm for our society if we are to maintain our standards of living and compete in a global economy.

In the K–10 chapter, I proposed an orientation course that would familiarize students with all their options for the future, the majors available to them, and the jobs they lead to. Here I recommend that we create a vocational bachelor's degree that can be obtained in three years. Again, this does not mean that currently there are no vocational schools. The few existing vocational schools are not part of a clear path to obtaining a degree and possessing a skill as I am suggesting. A three-year vocational bachelor's degree along with the reduction of K–12 to K–10 and the creation of a national high-school curriculum would mean that our students could graduate with a vocational bachelor's degree by the time they are nineteen years old. I also recommend that the three-year vocational bachelor's degree be free for all American citizens.

With this change, colleges will offer Bachelor of Science (BS), Bachelor of Arts (BA), and Bachelor of Vocation (BV) degrees. Only students who intend to continue on to graduate school for master's or doctorate degrees will attend a BS or BA program. Students who obtain BV degrees could enter the job market or continue on to BA, BS, and master's degrees if they wish. Depending on the major, it would then take one to two additional years to obtain a BA or BS, and three to four years to obtain a master's degree. A major difference between a vocational college and an academic one will be that the third year of a vocational college is a paid internship. Students must complete the internship in order to graduate.

The third-year internship means that BV graduates can immediately enter the job market since they possess hands-on experience, as opposed to those with BS or BA degrees, who may still need some apprenticeship after securing a job, unless they have had internships. This advantage entices some students to start with BV degrees even if they are planning to get their doctoral, master's, or even BS or BA degrees. I would expect that if such a system is adopted at some point in the future, BS and BA degrees would gradually become less popular, and students with a high-school diploma would attend either a three-year vocational school or a five-year graduate school to attain a master's degree.

The three-year vocational bachelor's degree should be offered free to US citizens but not to foreign students, who should pay as they do today. My proposed system would not add much cost, since the first two years of college would replace the last two years of high school, which we taxpayers currently pay for. The third year of vocational school would be a paid internship with minimum administrative costs.

This change could have a great effect on our country's educational system, since it would give every student the necessary knowledge to be an effective and skilled professional. Psychologically, it will also change how we view blue-collar and white-collar workers, since most blue-collar workers would now also hold a degree. This also allows those who earn a master's or doctoral degree to enter the job market and become productive two years sooner.

The only other change that I recommend is for our government to provide interest-free loans for students to obtain undergraduate and graduate degrees, as long as students commit to repaying the loan with a portion of their salaries as soon as they get a job. Many countries, such as Germany and Brazil, offer free or low-cost higher education while the total student loan stands at $1.2 trillion in the US, bearing 4.66% interest on average even at historically low interest rates.* *

Offering interest-free student loans is a step in the right direction, but still it does not address the runaway cost of higher education. A report by Higher Education Strategy Associates provides an in-depth analysis of affordability of higher education.* The report considers median income, education cost, living cost, grants, loans, and tax credits. It ranks the US twelfth or thirteenth out of fifteen countries when it considers these factors individually or combined. When all factors are considered, the US ranks behind England and Wales (11th), Latvia (10th), New Zealand (9th), France (8th), Canada (7th), Netherlands (6th), Denmark (5th), Germany (4th), Norway (3rd), Sweden (2nd), and Finland (1st).

The future of most American universities is not bright.* The cost of education has skyrocketed in recent decades, and our government has been forced to reduce educational subsidies. Additionally, new technologies have enabled universities to offer online courses, which allow students to choose the best lecturers from top universities and take courses anytime from anywhere. This arrangement also allows colleges to offer courses at reduced rates to many more attendees. This dynamic is changing our higher-education landscape and will put many less reputable colleges out of business.

We cannot prevent these changes, and we should not want to stop them. Instead, we should consider what lies ahead and direct these changes to our advantage. First, our government should offer standardized tests, certifications, and accreditations for online courses. This would validate and rank various online courses, making it simpler to obtain a degree.

Second, universities should change their curricula to become much more efficient and affordable. Moreover, reputable universities offering online courses can use the higher online profit margins to offer less expensive on-campus courses.

Third, the government should remove all subsidies for all colleges, except for providing zero-interest student higher-education loans and free three-year vocational bachelor's degrees. Once K–12 is restructured to K–10, the facilities that previously served grades 11 and 12 could be used for the first two years of the three-year vocational bachelor's program. Depending on the school districts, they may either offer BV programs in addition to high-school diplomas or make financial arrangements with colleges to do so. The same is true for staffing, even though some high-school teachers would not be qualified to teach college-level courses. The deficiency in qualification may be gradually alleviated through incentives for teachers to become certified to teach college-level courses. Incentives should be also given to colleges that now have little chance of surviving so that they can make improvements and offer such certifications.* This requires some work, which is expected when changing an archaic system of education into one fit for the twenty-first century.

19

Gun Politics

★ ★ ★ ★

believe that the Constitution and its amendments were created to protect our freedom. They were written to ensure
that the tools necessary to protect our freedom would
be available to everyone. I believe that when the Second
Amendment was written, the right to bear arms was critical
to ensuring our freedom. Using this logic, what do you think
would be considered critical to our freedom today? In other
words, if the Constitution were written today, would we still
protect the right to bear arms? I don't think so. I believe that,
if the founders were present today, they would be more concerned about protecting net neutrality, the principle that all
data on the Internet is treated equally and provided at the
same rate regardless of its origin, destination, content, or mode
of communication, rather than about the right to bear arms.

There are those who stick to their guns (pun intended)
because they do not trust our government. Some level of distrust is perhaps not only necessary but also healthy. The real

question is what one does with such distrust. If you own a gun due to such distrust, you may find some of my suggestions more effective to channel your distrust than owning a gun. The day that you need a gun to protect your freedom, you will find out that the battle for freedom is already lost.

While I do not believe that guns play any role in preserving our freedom, I also believe that gun rights have been too ingrained into our culture to be removed. Our rights are not absolute and must be balanced against each other. I should have the right to send my kids to school without worrying about whether or not they will get shot on the way to school or, even worse, at school! Our law enforcement agencies also have the right and duty to protect us without being fought by machine guns. We have to balance our rights.

If we are going to maintain our right to bear arms, we must balance that right with others' right to safety. People should feel safe knowing that only a sane, law-abiding citizen can obtain a gun, and that, if a gun is used in a crime, we can figure out to whom that gun belongs. I believe that available technology allows and can help us maintain this balance.

I propose that all guns be manufactured with biometric sensors, in such a fashion that a gun will not operate if the sensor is removed, or without its registered user's biometrics. In addition, bullets will identify the gun and hence its owner, who must provide a photo ID and clean bill of mental health upon its purchase. Finally, unregistered guns without biometric sensors would be banned, gun manufacturers would have a period to produce these new guns, and gun owners will, likewise, have a period to register their old guns or trade them for new ones.

Using existing biometric technology, guns could be pro-grammed to require validation every so often, depending on the credentials of a user. For example, a police officer may need to validate his gun every twenty-four hours. This simply means that when the gun recognizes its owner's biometrics, i.e. fingerprints, it is enabled for twenty-four hours before requiring another validation.

Today, the matching of a bullet with a gun is performed with a form of ballistic fingerprinting. This is a forensic sci-ence that utilizes the fact that each gun creates unique pat-terns on a bullet as the bullet goes through the grooves of the gun's barrel. However, this method is only useful when inves-tigators have the bullet and the gun to determine a positive or negative match. The bullet cannot be used to identify the gun if the gun is not present. A way around this is to collect infor-mation about a bullet fired from a gun before the gun is sold. This information is stored in a database. However, existing efforts to do this have not proven successful.*

The methodology I suggest is more like matching an email with its author, in which one can determine the author of the email with only the email. In this metaphor, a bul-let (email) would lead to the gun (device the email was writ-ten on) and the gun owner (the credential used to send the email). As with email, it may require some forensic work, but it would be highly accurate.

To achieve this, a technology called micro-stamping can be used.* It is essentially the same as ballistic fingerprinting, except that the barrel of the gun is engraved by laser. This microscopic engraving stamps the bullets with an ID unique to the gun. This ID is stored in a database along with the gun's make, model, and serial number. Upon the sale of a gun, the database would capture the gun owner's information.

We have the technology to allow the safe use of guns, to solve more crimes more quickly and less expensively, to feel safer in our homes and in public, and to increase the safety of our law enforcement agents, and it's time to use it.

20

Illicit Drugs

★ ★ ★ ★

Read the fine print that accompanies your prescription drugs and you may as well be reading the script of a horror movie with warnings about the risk of hair and teeth falling out, going blind, and of course death. So danger is certainly not a reason to keep illegal drugs illegal. Then the reason must be some of their habit-forming properties, right? That argument, of course, holds only if everything else that is habit-forming were illegal—that is, alcohol, tobacco, smartphones, social media, and video games, to name a few. Drugs can, in fact, destroy a person, a family, and an entire segment of our society, and they do so—causing immense damage to the poor and disadvantaged segment of the population.

I believe that there are three primary reasons why illicit drugs are illegal. The first reason is that we believe they are harmful, and indeed they are. Drugs are also illegal because they are associated with various crimes. However, most drug related crimes occur as the result of the illegality of drugs. If I compare the harm of illicit drugs to a bee sting, their illegality would be the body's overreaction to the sting. The crimes resulting from the illegality of drugs are a much bigger issue than the drugs themselves. By criminalizing illicit drugs, we have turned a potentially manageable social issue into an enormous socioeconomic one.

In general, we associate drugs with violence and crime, problems that the majority of us hear about in the news but have no firsthand experience with. When we fear something that we do not know much about—and truthfully we do not want to know about drugs—it's easier for us to keep our distance and remain oblivious to the problem. We have seemingly handled the issue by making it illegal, routinely handing out progressively harsher punishments to violators. The illegality of illicit drugs and the violence and crime associated with them create an opportunity for criminals to make money, and lots of it. This reinforces the illegality of drugs, and ensures that the problem remains. As long as drugs are illegal, money will be made, and as long as money is made, drugs will be illegal, and the vicious cycle will continue. In short, by making drugs illegal, we have not solved the problem. Instead, we have created a financial incentive for dealers and illicit drug producers to perpetuate their careers—that is the third primary reason for the criminalization of illicit drugs.

Drug are also criminalized because of increased public spending on health-related issues and the self-destructive behavior of the addicts, among other reasons. Again, in both cases, there are plenty of examples of other activities that can increase healthcare costs and are harmful but legal—drinking, smoking, and eating junk food to name a few.

To make matters worse, our efforts to control illicit drugs, the so-called war on drugs, have miserably failed. A Stanford University article best describes our efforts:

> America is at war. We have been fighting drug abuse for almost a century. Four Presidents have personally waged war on drugs. Unfortunately, it is a war that we are losing. Drug abusers continue to fill our courts, hospitals, and prisons. The drug trade causes violent crime that ravages our neighborhoods. Children of drug abusers are neglected, abused, and even abandoned. The only beneficiaries of this war are organized crime members and drug dealers.*

Let's ignore the fact that drugs are harmful for a moment and imagine that we could walk into a liquor store, show our ID, and buy any type of drugs. In this scenario, what would the incentive be for a drug dealer to sell drugs? Would there be a need to buy arms, and where would the money to acquire arms come from? Why would anyone push drugs at our schools? For what reasons would drug cartels exist? Would anyone ever be killed in a drug deal? Would our prisons still be overcrowded? And would we be spending millions fighting the drug cartels? No, we wouldn't.

The truth is that drugs are harmful. But so are alcohol and saturated fat at various degrees. Harmful should not mean illegal. The fact that drugs are harmful is a health matter. Rather than permitting drug lords to generate enough profit to afford armies and fight us, or allowing drugs to be manufactured in illegal basement labs with untested ingredients, we should take over the production and distribution of drugs as we have successfully done with alcohol. Taxes collected from the sales of drugs will be commensurate with the level of burden that drugs impose on our society and would be used to rehabilitate drug addicts, and to campaign against and educate our population about the perils of drug use.

To review our illicit drug policy, we must differentiate soft drugs such as marijuana from hard drugs such as cocaine and heroin. In some countries as well as some states in the US, possession of small amounts of soft drugs such as weed is legal. On the other hand, Portugal is the only country that has allowed possession of any drug, soft or hard, since 2001.

While legalizing all drugs, hard or soft, may ultimately be the solution, I believe that our society is not prepared to handle legalization of hard drugs. What I suggest is the legalization of soft drugs and decriminalization of hard ones. When legalizing soft drugs, I suggest that they be treated similarly to alcohol with the exception that they may not be consumed in public places, whether these places are privately or publicly owned. As it is with alcohol, public consumption of drugs may encourage nonusers to start consuming drugs.

Since I suggest that hard drugs be decriminalized and soft drugs be legalized, I would like to take a moment to define these terms. With the exception of public consumption, the legalization of soft drugs would work very similarly to the way alcohol does today; that is, there would be rules around their sales, distribution, and consumption. For example, one must be twenty-one years of age to legally buy and consume soft drugs.

On the other hand, decriminalization of hard drugs means that one cannot legally sell, distribute, or consume them, but violators would be fined or have driving privileges suspended. These penalties and fines would vary depending on the violation. In all cases, any discovery of hard drugs would result in confiscation.

The legalization of soft drugs should be closely controlled and monitored at the federal level, otherwise various states will end up with laws that can have adverse effects. Pricing of soft drugs is a good example of what should be closely monitored and controlled at the federal level. If the price is too high, the black markets will remain and legalization would become ineffective or even harmful. If the price is too low, it may encourage current users to consume more. Inconsistent pricing from state to state would lead to criminals stepping in to take advantage of price differences—supplying soft drugs from lower-price states to higher-price ones. Over time, state legislators may forget the reasons for legalizing soft drugs and view the taxation as another revenue source. For all these reasons, the federal government should take the lead, draw up policies, and set the standards on this legalization. In the journal *Substance Use and Misuse*, Anne Line Bretteville-Jensen offers an informative cost-benefit analysis on legalization of drugs.*

We cannot stigmatize our drug addicts as outcasts and criminals. We need to treat them as sick members of our population who desperately need our help. Throwing them in prison is not fixing the issue; it is hurting us. When we do this, we turn sick people into criminals and we pay for their room and board, often for too long. Worse yet, we teach them how to be real criminals while in prison. Instead, we must legalize soft drugs, decriminalize possession and consumption of hard drugs in small amounts, and manage our social problems.

21

Prostitution

★ ★ ★ ★

Similar to illicit drugs, the illegality of prostitution could be justified if it did not lead to worse problems, and if it were effective. Unfortunately, the illegality of prostitution does lead to other serious issues, including abuse and human trafficking, and is ineffective.

Prostitution is illegal in all states but Nevada, yet its market's size was estimated at $14 billion annually nationwide, which *The Economist* considers an underestimate.* An analysis of 190,000 sex workers in eighty-four cities in twelve countries revealed the US has the highest number of sex workers. These statistics simply show that the illegalization of prostitution has not stopped it.

On the other hand, its legalization may have some unexpected positive consequences. For example, the number of reported gonorrhea and rape cases declined when Rhode Island unintentionally decriminalized indoor prostitution between 2003 and 2009.*

Prostitution has always existed and most likely always will, but when it is illegal, it is pushed underground. As such, it leaves room for abuse, STDs, violence, and human trafficking, among other problems. Criminalization of the sex trade pushes its workers to the margins of our society—making them less likely to seek care or report abuse to the police, fearing arrest.

Legalizing prostitution removes most health and social issues from the equation, and allows it to be regulated. As reprehensible as it may sound, regulating prostitution will remove abuse, suffering, and distress from the system, and it would allow resources spent preventing it to be used on issues more critical to our society.

The global market of human trafficking is estimated to be as high as $32 billion, involving around 800,000 people who are trafficked across borders and millions more who are traded domestically each year. Eighty percent of those traded internationally are women forced into some form of prostitution.* In the US, these abuses are less likely to be reported due to the illegality of the act, but since 2012, 10,755 cases have been reported.* Contrary to what one might expect for the US, over 76% of 2014's reported sex trafficking cases involved a US citizen or lawful permanent resident. Legalizing prostitution does not eliminate the human trafficking, but rather makes it easier for sex workers to seek help and for sex seekers to report it.

Making illicit drugs and prostitution taboos does not cause them to simply go away. We must manage them. The legalization of soft drugs and prostitution also generates taxes, which in turn can be used to address the social burden and immorality of both. The money collected should be used not only for enforcement and advertisement against these vices, but also to control child pornography. I believe that child pornography is among the biggest social issues we deal with. The simple reason is the ease and convenience with which it can be produced. Since underage pornography has proliferated with the advent of technology and personal computers, the solution may also be found through the use of technology.

To begin with, the FBI or other appointed agencies should develop a program to systematically run facial recognition on pornographic media against global databases of missing and exploited children. The facial recognition technology can flag matches for further investigation.

Additionally, there should be a Safe Seal that adult sites can obtain to identify them as safe sites. Such sites must run their content through a governing body to ensure that their materials do not include child pornography. Facial recognition can also be used to electronically exclude known adult participants from the screening process and award their material a Safe Seal. The Safe Seal provides a legitimate outlet available to law-abiding participants.

I am sure that even more can be done to curb child pornography once this initiative has begun. In the end, nothing entirely eliminates child pornography, but using technology will allow us to focus our resources on it and can make it less widespread. In short, we should legalize prostitution, control porn, and redirect our resources to reduce child pornography and human trafficking.

22

Private Prisons

★ ★ ★ ★

I f there is a list of tasks that must be performed by our government and not by the private sector, managing our prisons must be on it. Prisons operated by corporations have the same objectives as hotels do; that is, to have as many guests as possible, keep these guests as long as possible, and ensure that they return often. The occupancy rate for both hotels and private prisons determines their profit. Hotels increase their occupancy rates by providing a memorable stay. Since criminals do not voluntarily check into prison or have a choice of prison, a private prison can only grow by having more criminals or by ensuring that criminals receive longer sentences for their crimes.

But private prisons do not make criminals, so what role can they play in achieving their financial goals? In the past decade, they spent $45 million in campaign donations and lobbying to push legislation seeking to increase sentences and incarcerate more people.* Private prisons hold about half of detained immigrants at a cost of $166 a night. The Federal Bureau of Prisons is paying $5.1 billion to hold more than 23,000 criminal immigrants. The market cap of the top two private prisons is $6.2 billion. According to Yahoo:

> Some estimate that the crackdown on undocumented immigrants will lead to 14,000 more inmates annually with 80% of that business going to private prisons.*

The following excerpt from an annual report by a top private prison should demonstrate why the goals of such companies are contrary to what we should achieve as a society:

> The demand for our facilities and services could be adversely affected by the relaxation of enforcement efforts, leniency in conviction or parole standards and sentencing practices or through the decriminalization of certain activities that are currently proscribed by our criminal laws. For instance, any changes with respect to drugs and controlled substances or illegal immigration could affect the number of persons arrested, convicted, and sentenced, thereby potentially reducing demand for correctional facilities to house them.*

As a society, we ought to do a better job of understanding the role that various entities play in our society and ensure that they serve their intended purposes. What is the role and purpose of a prison? Why do we put people in prison? The simple answer is to punish them. However, when we imprison someone, we are not just punishing that person. We are also taking on the burden of sponsoring a complete stranger. We pay for his or her shelter, food, safety, and health. As a punishment, we turn an independent adult into a dependent person to whom we become a provider. We do this even though some of us cannot afford to provide a comparable level of service for our own parents. So when we imprison someone, we penalize not only them but also ourselves.

This is not to say that we shouldn't put criminals in prison, but we should use imprisonment more discriminately and ensure its effectiveness. To maintain a just society, we have to use prisons, but their primary purpose should be to influence the convict to repent, become a law-abiding citizen, and leave prison as soon as possible. We will discuss reducing the number of prisoners later.

Prisons can be effective by helping to change criminals into law-abiding citizens, not by turning petty criminals into felons. Recidivism is defined as one's relapse into criminal behavior. In one study, out of 404,638 prisoners, two-thirds of those released were rearrested within three years.* The recidivism rate was 76.6% within five years of release. When three out of four prisoners go back to prison after serving their sentence, our prisons are not effective. In order to be effective, all prisons must be fully operated by the government to ensure that there is an incentive to keep our prisons empty, not full. Next, we should do away with any law that requires our judges to deliver mandatory sentences, such as the three-strikes laws. Sentencing should be a function of the judiciary branch, not the legislative branch.

While in prison, our prisoners should either work or get educated. But we have to make sure that we compensate the prisoners at minimum wage, not at 25 cents per hour, and to treat them humanely.* Those who work can enjoy the incentives of better food or cells in addition to earning wages. Nothing is as effective as work in creating strong morals. Those who do not have a high-school diploma can earn one or learn a profession while doing time. Additionally, all prisoners must be taught about the nature of the crime they committed and how it affects their victims and society. An associate of mine pointed me to the Pre-Release and Reentry Services (PRRS) of Montgomery County, Maryland, as an example of what I am describing.* This is what PRRS states on its website:

> Participants are released from incarceration with employment, treatment, family support, and the Division saves taxpayer money, reduces institutional crowding, and reduces recidivism and victimization rates.

The recidivism rate of the PRRS is 40% lower than nationally measured rates. Imagine this at the national level.

23

Capital Punishment

★ ★ ★ ★

The punishment must fit the crime. Therefore, to uphold justice, a wide spectrum of punishments must be available. On one hand, this means that laws like the three-strikes law must be removed so that appropriate punishments can be handed out for misdemeanors. On the other hand, capital punishment should always be an option for capital crimes. Capital offenses mostly involve murders or deaths, as well as treason and espionage.

Capital punishment evokes our primal instinct to survive, and as such, there should be no replacement for it. The fear of death or execution is one of the strongest deterrents to committing murder. Without capital punishment, there is no fear of death, thus reducing a capital offense to a crime punishable by a potentially long imprisonment. Imprisonment is certainly a punishment, but not one that evokes our primal instincts of survival and therefore reluctance to commit a capital crime.

Not only should capital punishment be among the punishment options for capital crimes, the execution should be carried out as close to the date of the crime as possible so that it acts as a deterrent to others. If potential murderers believe that they will be dead next year should they commit a murder today, they would be much less inclined to commit that murder. However, if criminals believe that there is hardly any chance of capital punishment, or that they may have ten to twenty years to live prior to their execution, that primal fear of death may not be present. When death (by execution) is so far off in the future, it is a hardly a consideration—after all, we all eventually die. Therefore, for capital punishment to deter capital crimes, there must be a realistic chance that it will happen, and if it does, it must be carried out as promptly as possible. Of course, it would be impossible to carry out such a punishment within weeks of a crime, but there should be a guaranteed timeframe to ensure that a criminal is executed as soon as they are proven guilty beyond a reasonable doubt, and after reasonable appeals have been processed.

The opponents of capital punishment argue either that life is too precious to be taken away and that executions are too barbaric, or that capital punishment is irreversible should subsequent evidence show a convict to be innocent after his or her execution. The first argument is counterintuitive since the value of the victim's life was also precious, yet it was taken for two reasons: first, because it was clearly not valued by the murderer, and second, because in places where capital punishment does not exist, its absence has removed the primal fear of death from the equation. Without capital punishment, we are valuing the life of a murderer over the life of a victim.

If capital punishment is available and carried out swiftly, some murders may never occur in the first place.

To address the second argument, we must view capital punishment from another angle: opportunity cost. Today, life without parole (LWOP) is often used instead of capital punishment. LWOP works like this: one person deliberately murders another and is arrested for what is believed to be the worst possible crime. The criminal is then tried, convicted, sentenced, and incarcerated for fifty years. Edwin H. Sutherland, PhD, and Donald R. Cressey, PhD, wrote in their book *Criminology*:

> Being alive and having nothing better to do, [the criminal] will spend his time in prison conceiving of ever-new habeas corpus petitions, which being unlimited, in effect cannot be rejected as res judicata (a matter judged).

The annual cost for maintaining an inmate in California is $47,102, or $2.3 million over fifty years.* However, the opponents of capital punishment argue that the cost of maintaining an inmate on death row is much higher—$137,102 a year—and in California, prisoners spend twenty years on average in prison before they are executed, totaling $2.7 million. The death penalty also has a much higher upfront cost than LWOP due to more complex trial procedures. In short, the cost of having an inmate on death row for twenty years is much higher than having an inmate in prison for fifty years. However, with what I suggest, an inmate should not be on death row for more than two to five years. This would reduce the total cost of keeping an inmate on death row to $675,000. Even after adding the initial cost of seeking the death penalty to the cost of incarceration, capital punishment costs at least a million dollars less than LWOP.

With this in mind, and looking at capital punishment from the perspective of opportunity cost, we have to understand how many lives we can save if we execute a convicted murderer in a timely manner and spend the savings elsewhere. We could invest the money in helping cancer patients, for example. Not considering the opportunity cost lead to not sparing any amount of money in order to preserve the life of a convicted murderer, while at the same time we allow countless people to die because we do not have the money to treat their cancer, feed them, or find a cure for their disease. In short, as the late Mr. Spock put it, "The needs of the many outweigh the needs of the few." In this case, a few too many murderers.

To ensure that capital punishment is available and carried out swiftly, we also need to ensure that our justice system works flawlessly. Many convictions rely on the testimony of witnesses. However, some witnesses for the state testify after receiving plea bargains from prosecutors, accepting reduced sentences in exchange for testimony against a defendant. The situation with cases involving plea bargains become even worse when mandatory sentences are available to prosecutors, since these laws practically take the judge and the jury out of the process. With mandatory sentences, such as the three-strikes law, prosecutors can charge the witness with a lesser crime that automatically qualifies the witness for lesser punishment in exchange for the witness's testimony. This scenario can become worse still if prosecutors threaten to charge the witness with a bigger crime, one that carries a more severe punishment, unless the witness testifies against the defendant.

It is not hard to imagine that a witness would provide false testimony either due to fear of being charged with a bigger crime or in the hope of being charged with a lesser crime. While I believe that all mandatory sentences should be removed and that prosecutors should be barred from striking plea bargains, we should, at least, dismiss the testimony of any witness who is subject to a mandatory sentence or plea bargain in trials involving capital punishment. We will talk more about mandatory sentences in another chapter.

In summary, I suggest that plea bargains be prohibited when capital punishment is sought, and that capital punishment be available and swiftly executed to reduce costs.

24

White-Collar Crimes

★ ★ ★ ★

When we think of crime, we may instinctively think of blue-collar crimes—crimes that primitively threaten our safety and security. But as tragic as they may be, these crimes affect a small portion of the population with each occurrence. On the other hand, white-collar crimes can have much more devastating effects on a much larger segment of our society. The actions of a single drug addict who is imprisoned for drug possession have far less impact on our society than a man in a suit and tie who relaxes the lending criteria on mortgages, or fails to lower credit ratings when warranted, or does not issue a product recall when necessary.

Typically, drug addicts suffer from addiction, a medical condition, and most often they are victims of their circumstances. The number of people directly affected by them—their family, friends, and significant others—may number in the dozens, and their addiction's cost to society is limited to hundreds of thousands of dollars. On the other hand, mortgage-backed securities caused the 2008 financial meltdown and cost the middle class billions. Predatory lending practices destroyed the lives of hundreds of thousands of families, but how many of those predatory lenders were indicted or received life sentences? In these cases, investigations typically take years, along with millions of dollars, only to sentence one person to a minimum prison sentence or a fine. As a result of the 2008 financial meltdown, a single banker was sentenced to thirty months of imprisonment.* Imagine if a mandatory sentence of one year were imposed for every $100,000 used in a bribe, embezzled, or acquired by fraud. While I do not advocate mandatory sentences, such a practice could drastically reduce the amount of white-collar crimes. (As previously noted, I am categorically against mandatory sentences since I believe that a judge and a jury should always ultimately have the power to decide the outcome of a case.)

The point of the suggestion to legalize soft drugs and prostitution is to reserve resources spent ineffectively in pursuing frivolous crimes and to instead spend resources and effort investigating crimes that have a much broader impact on society. Imagine that an executive at a credit-rating agency had been imprisoned for maintaining high credit ratings for the mortgage-backed securities responsible for the 2008 financial meltdown. Other executives would think long and hard before playing a role in the next financial crisis.

The interesting aspect of imprisoning white-collar criminals is that they have much more to lose by going to prison than blue-collar criminals do. Hence, imprisonment is a much more effective punishment for white-collar crimes.

25

One-Time Parole

★ ★ ★ ★

One out of every hundred adults in the United States is incarcerated.* We have 2.4 million people in prisons, and as of June 2012, there are 700,000 in jails, and another 22,000 being held as immigration detainees. We also account for 25% of the world's prisoners, while our population is only 5% of the world. We drastically need to reduce the number of people in our prisons. The rate of incarceration will undoubtedly drop once prostitution and soft drugs are legalized and hard drugs are decriminalized, as discussed in earlier chapters.

We can further decrease that rate by redefining statutory rape to eliminate cases where the age difference of the parties involved is five years or less. That would mean that a voluntary act between a twenty-year-old (an adult) and a fifteen-year-old (a minor) would not be considered statutory rape. Rape is the second most violent crime in our society. Treating sex between two young adults with a small age difference as a crime in the class of rape only hurts our society by minimizing the heinousness of rape.

Decriminalizing illicit drugs and prostitution, redefining statutory rape where the age difference is fewer than five years, and enforcing capital punishment all free up our resources. These resources can then be utilized to toughen our stance on white-collar crimes and crimes against children, such as child pornography.

Out of about 71,000 juveniles, around 11,600 are imprisoned for technical violations of their probation or parole terms, and not because they have committed new crimes.* This is another area that we can improve on. We will discuss revisiting the laws in the chapter Sunset Clause that will lead to fewer arrests. Eliminating private prisons, as we discussed earlier, reduces lobbying, which could in turn lower incarceration rates. Although these changes will drastically reduce incarceration, we must still deal with our current prison population.

To fix this problem, I suggest that we provide a one-time parole to current prisoners based on certain criteria determined by a panel of judges. Such criteria, for example, would exclude hardcore felons such as murderers and rapists, but include everyone else such as those incarcerated for statutory rape and reduce their sentences. The reduction would be handed down according to the nature of the crime committed. The reduction should be either a percentage or a fixed number of years off the original sentence.

These suggestions would ensure that the number of prisoners will drop and that those remaining in prison actually belong there. Additionally, the deprivatization of prisons ensures that there is no incentive to keep prisoners in prison. The reform would also make certain that prisoners understand their crime, and that they receive an education or learn a skill while in prison.

26

Border Control and Immigration

★ ★ ★ ★

We are a nation of immigrants, but we are a nation first and immigrants second. What defines a nation? Its physical borders, its language, its laws, its history, its culture, its compassion or aggressiveness? Perhaps all of these and more. For a nation to prosper, it must protect its border, preserve its language and culture, and enforce its laws. There were over ten million illegal immigrants living in the US in 2013. The term "illegal immigrant" states two simple nonpolitical facts: that we cannot control our borders and that there are millions of immigrants living in the country, in violation of US laws.*

A sovereign nation must control its borders. By not doing this, our nation not only encourages breaking the law but also jeopardizes the lives of people who attempt to cross our borders every day. It is both interesting and puzzling to realize how often we get involved to protect another nation's sovereignty, yet we fail to control our own borders. A nation's sovereignty starts with its borders. If we close our borders to illegal immigration, violators will quickly learn that attempting to cross the border is futile and will gradually stop trying. Human trafficking, drug and weapon smuggling, and the illegal flow of currency will be drastically reduced, resulting in fewer crimes, less corruption, and hence, safer cities.

After tightening our border control, we have to address the over ten million illegal immigrants already in our country. Keeping their unlawful status will not help anyone nor will it lead to a resolution. Providing amnesty to current illegal immigrants converts an underground economy into one that you and I can benefit from. It eliminates the crime and abuse associated with illegal immigration and allows illegal immigrants to carry their weight by becoming documented and paying taxes.

This is no easy feat, since each person must be subjected to background screening to distinguish true criminals from those whose only crime is following their hopes and dreams. The criminals must be deported while others would go through the necessary procedures to become legal and pay their back taxes. With the right planning, we can transform over ten million illegal immigrants into millions of law-abiding citizens.

I must also point out that illegal immigration only accounts for about a quarter of total immigrants—meaning that plenty of people do migrate here legally. Around 40.8 million people, or 13% of the US population, are immigrants (foreign born), of whom over 10 million are here illegally. Both the number of immigrants in the country and the percentage of our population composed of immigrants have increased. From 1970 to 2000, the number of immigrants in the country rose from 9.6 million to 31.1 million. *

The current trend in immigration is for families to come to the US, give birth, and become entitled to the privileges of having an American child. This trend is known as "birth tourism." According to CNN Money, 10,000 Chinese women gave birth in the US in 2012, more than double the 4,200 in 2008.* I believe that citizenship status should be obtained honestly. Arriving in the US illegally or on a tourist visa intending to give birth should not qualify the child to that status. One way to address this is to require one year of residency for the parents when they are not Americans or permanent residents of the US. Exceptions must be made for those who seek asylum and cannot control the timing of their migration. With this policy, a baby born to foreign parents in the US would not automatically become an American citizen until his or her parents prove that they had been in the US for at least one year prior to the birth.

President Obama has an immigration plan that paves the way to transition over ten million illegal immigrants to legal status. When illegal immigrants become legal, they vote overwhelmingly for the Democratic Party.* This may play a role in creating the plan, but it does not change the need for such a plan. However, it would be counterproductive unless we first control our borders; otherwise, we would be providing more incentives for immigrants to cross our borders illegally.

27

Sunset Clause

★ ★ ★ ★

Our laws are simply the accumulation of rules that have been enacted as needed. Over time, layers upon layers of rules have been drafted to address our needs. The way our laws develop is like starting with a one-bedroom apartment building and gradually evolving it into a thousand-room hotel. The maze of rules works beautifully for the hotel staff, who are familiar with the layout, but not for the guests. This complexity allows lawyers (and those who can afford lawyers) to use the laws to their advantage.

While we still enjoy one of the most just systems in the world, this complexity allows money to trump justice. To make a simple point, if a Fortune 500 company asks a small business to stop using a brand, the small business has two options: give in, or fight back until it runs out of money. Who has the right to the name is never the issue, but how much money can be spent to defend it is. Some of you may recall the case between the government and Microsoft regarding whether Microsoft should allow the Netscape browser to fairly compete against Microsoft's Internet Explorer, which came with the Microsoft operating system. By the time the case was settled, Netscape had lost its momentum and its share of the market.

I believe that every new law should include an expiration date of one, three, five, or ten years. If the new law is controversial or unproven, a shorter term such as one or three years can be applied; otherwise, longer terms can be used. To prevent politics from deciding the term, we can link the expiration date to the relative number of votes in Congress. In other words, if a bill has bipartisan support, it gets a longer term. For example, a bill that gets at least 60% of votes from each party could qualify to become law for ten years, whereas a bill that gets 70% of one party's votes, but only 20% from the other, would last only three years before it is considered for renewal.

Regardless of its term, every law should expire. The deadlines would be monitored before their expiration dates, allowing public discussion and voting by Congress on whether or not to renew it. The ongoing process of renewal and the related public discussions ensure that our laws stay current with the changes in our society. This would enable our laws to remain suitable for current issues. Expiration dates would also be assigned to every existing law. This does not mean that every existing law would expire, rendering us lawless. To the contrary, it would force us to review every law and determine whether it is still valid, if it needs to be revised, or if it should be allowed to expire. To handle existing laws, we'd declare that all laws over a hundred years old will expire in ten years. At the other extreme, we might assign an additional twenty-year lifespan to every law less than ten years old. Similarly, we would assign expiration dates for laws between ten and a hundred years old. In this manner, older laws would be reviewed sooner than newer ones, and every law would be reviewed sooner or later.

This breathes fresh air into our justice system, prepares our laws for new generations, promotes public awareness, and, of course, brings more clarity as to what's right or wrong. While it does not change the role of money in our justice system, this would make its presence a little less important. Public debates and discussions of new or existing laws create familiarity and exposure while educating the public, and that is a win for everyone. As a society, we lose when we are not informed or involved.

28

Pit Stop 2

★ ★ ★ ★

After ensuring that we have the right people in office and informed citizens, we turned our attention to issues that can once again set us apart as a model nation to the world. We reduced the legal voting age to sixteen in order to put younger generations in charge of their destinies. Then we reduced the K–12 education system to K–10 and changed the curriculum in recognition of the fact that most primary and secondary schools fail to achieve their purpose. We also introduced a revised and standardized national curriculum to ensure that every high-school graduate learns what matters. We added Spanish as a second language, recognizing the growing Latino population. We introduced a new Bachelor of Vocation (BV) degree, which can be obtained in three years, and made it free so that almost everyone can have a bachelor's degree by age 19. More importantly, we made such degrees available in a broad range of professions to ensure that everyone has a practical skill, unless they are planning to pursue a more advanced degree. These changes allow new generations to become productive earlier, close the social and income inequality gap that can be attributed to inconsistencies in the current K-12 education, and make knowing a practical skill to secure a job a reality.

To address gun control, we argued that they are no longer critical to our freedom, since despite guns being easily available, our freedom has long been deteriorating. Although I believe that guns only hurt us, we compromised to allow guns under the following conditions: guns must be biometrically registered to a user so only the registered user can trigger the gun. Also, bullets must be able to be matched to a gun, which an owner can only obtain with any government-issued photo ID and a clean bill of mental health. Finally, a ban on old, unregistered guns must go into effect within a reasonable timeframe such as three to five years.

Addressing other issues that mostly target minorities, we legalized soft drugs and prostitution and decriminalized hard drugs with the understanding that keeping them illegal only harms our society, and that the money spent fighting drugs could be spent more effectively fighting cancer, for example. We ensured that our prisons are efficient at turning criminals into productive, law-abiding citizens, and we eliminated all private prisons. We suggested that capital punishment remain available as a possible sentence and that it be carried out swiftly. Then we provided one-time parole to make up for our erroneous practices and our wrong stance on drugs. In doing so, we toughened the laws on white-collar crimes.

We noted two key tasks for which our federal government is responsible: protecting our borders and enforcing our laws.

The number of illegal immigrants and the amount of drugs and guns entering our country each year indicate that we are failing on both fronts. In response, we supported a form of amnesty for current illegal immigrants, but only after our government can control our borders.

Finally, we introduced a sunset clause for every law to reduce the influence of wealth on the justice system, to make laws simpler and more transparent, and to create public awareness of existing laws.

29

Capping Capitalism

★ ★ ★ ★

B y now we have some understanding of what a billion is, but let's see if we can really understand the scope of it. Here are examples to illustrate what I mean by scope. Suppose that we are throwing a party and plan to prepare meals for our guests. If we are inviting one couple for lunch, this would be a party with a small scope and would be relatively easy to handle. If, on the other hand, we host twenty people from out of town for Thanksgiving dinner, the party's scope is certainly larger. If we consider hosting a convention at a Las Vegas mega-hotel, well, that is a whole different scope.

To understand how large the scope of a billion dollars is, let's consider real estate, since, for most people, a house is the largest purchase they will ever make. Let's say that homes have an average price of $250,000. If we have one, well, we just live in it and take care of it. When we have two houses, we need to maintain both and probably rent out one of them. If we have ten of them, we'll probably need a license to rent and manage them. With ten rental houses, on average, a lease would expire roughly each month, and some repairs would be necessary on average once a year. So there is more involved with owning ten houses. If we have a hundred houses, reaching the size of a subdivision, then our issues would be, of course, much larger. We would have agreements with real-estate agents to buy, sell, or lease properties; agreements with contractors to maintain them; interior decorators to stage them for sale or lease; and suppliers and insurance companies to provide us volume discount services. All this may require an in-house counsel and one or two full-time repairmen. We would also need to deal with other issues such as utilities, bylaws, property maintenance, street maintenance, and so on. We may even need our own security guards. So the scope of owning a hundred houses is much larger and more elaborate than owning one or two.

When we have a thousand houses, the scope is not just larger, it's completely different. Going back to the example of our small party, having just one couple over, if the weather is cool, we may need to keep the house warm. If we are hosting a big Thanksgiving dinner, amid the hustle and bustle of twenty guests, we might keep the heat down. When the scope is large enough, the dynamic, the issues, and the way to deal with them all become different. With a thousand houses, there is much more at stake, so we must pay attention to issues that we would have otherwise considered out of our control. Our legal counsel and advisors might become involved with property assessments to keep our property taxes in check, work directly with the utility companies to ensure that everything functions smoothly, get involved with zoning and city planners to ensure that our properties benefit from any changes, advocate for public transportation and better roads for our residents, and ensure that city councils and mayors agree with our plans. If we wanted to, we could provide our own insurance to our properties, and perhaps even enter the business of lending money. We would then be engaged in the insurance and banking businesses, in addition to real estate and construction. So by virtue of owning a thousand houses, we are now in at least four different industries.

A billion dollars could buy four thousand quarter-million-dollar properties, and the top three billionaires on the *Forbes* list can collectively buy 855,000 of these houses.* Assuming four people per household, this community would accommodate 3.2 million people. The third-largest city in the US, Chicago, had a population of 2.7 million in 2012. The point I am trying to make is that the scope of the playing field for billionaires is so large that they are forced to influence politics in order to do business. That is the nature of a billion dollars, and that is why we must do something in order to restore and preserve our freedom.

This is why I believe that we need to put a cap on capitalism. The question is: How much is enough, and how do we cap it? So first, let's define what capping capitalism entails. Capping capitalism means placing a threshold on the net worth of an individual so that the individual's wealth no longer grows, or grows at a drastically slower rate. Keep in mind that we are talking about someone's hard-earned money and not the wealth of a third-world dictator. I believe that this cap should be set in a way that a billionaire's lifestyle does not change. Bear in mind that I am referring to lifestyle, which is determined by spending, and not necessarily by ownership. If lifestyle were determined by ownership, no amount of money would ever be enough, since there are never enough palaces, jets, yachts, islands, and other luxuries that one can own.

When it comes to spending, $250 million in net worth should create a level of affordability that would not change with additional wealth. But the level that I am recommending as the cap is not $250 million, but a billion dollars. Why? Because I believe that for billionaires, having a billion is a must to keep their membership in the exclusive billionaires' club. But how do billionaires maintain their wealth at a billion dollars? I would imagine that billionaires can find many ways to keep their wealth at a billion.

First, they could give the excess to charity or set up their own foundations, like the Bill and Melinda Gates Foundation, to serve society. Besides the obvious benefits of this move, there are practical reasons. Often, there is not enough liquid wealth, such as cash on hand, to be given, so shares of companies, whether public or private, can be transferred to charities without the need for liquidation.

Second, they can use the extra wealth to sponsor projects for the country's infrastructure, such as toll-free highways, bridges, high-speed trains, or electrical grids. The possibilities are endless. Billionaires could also put their names on these projects as a reminder of their achievements.

Third, they could give wealth to others, so that their cousins, uncles, aunts, or total strangers could become millionaires or billionaires, too. The only caveat here is that they should not be able to form collaborative groups to control funds even though the money has been given away; otherwise, capping capitalism would be pointless. Controlling funds can be achieved in various ways depending on the structure. If funds have been transferred to a foundation, the donors can continue serving the foundation. For such foundations, I suggest that the board of directors manage the foundation while allowing the donors to serve the foundation if so desired. If the money has been given away to family members or strangers, it would be possible for the donor to remain the money manager. Donors must not manage donated money so that the giving serves its purpose.

If billionaires do not cap their wealth, the excess may be collected as taxes in a special fund that we could call the Cap Capitalism Fund. This fund will be used to make up for any deficit in funding for the National Healthcare System, the Social Security trust fund, second homes, or as a reserve for any future deficit in these funds. We will discuss these programs in their respective chapters. While some of you may think that there is no precedent for my suggestions, in 1944 we taxed income over $200,000 at 94%.* The growth of billionaires' net worth is considered income and should be subjected to such taxation for the greater good of the country.

Another question is whether such a cap would apply to current billionaires or just to the people who attain this status after the policy is established. Of course, the preference is that the cap would apply to both current and new billionaires. However, we would have a much better chance of implementing the cap if we applied such a rule only to newly created billionaires. By doing so, we practically close the membership to the multi-billionaires' club, making it even more exclusive. The existing multi-billionaires would become a force to help in capping capitalism and preventing others from amassing more than a billion dollars since this would give them an advantage.

If a limit on wealth is ever implemented in the US, we should also consider revising our rules with regard to global wealth and close some loopholes related to wealth. We could influence other countries to consider similar laws and change the global picture of how wealth is concentrated.

If we actually were to apply such a rule to existing billionaires, there would be a large surplus of funds that could address many of our national issues. However, unless this rule obtained support from some existing billionaires, it would have no chance of gaining political traction. For those of you who may think that this suggestion is a form of communism, I would first say that there are about 250 billionaires in China and Russia combined.* And second, if the only difference between capitalism and communism were capping one's wealth at a measly billion, perhaps communism would not be such a bad thing!

30

Banking and the US Monetary System

★ ★ ★ ★

e previously discussed how money, politics, and information form the tripod of power. We argued that billionaires are a new threat to our freedom, but we have not yet discussed a traditional threat: bankers.

Bankers govern our financial system. The houses we live in, the cars we drive, the businesses we work for, and (for some of us) our daily expenses, from one paycheck to another, are all financed by banks. In fact, the banking system is so convenient that we no longer need to carry cash. It allows us to have our earnings deposited directly into our bank accounts, from which the banks pay our bills on our behalf. If we happen to save money, they provide us with options to invest it. We love convenience, and banks do not leave a lot to be desired.

Of course, with all the convenience that we get from banks comes a price: our freedom and our wealth. If you were caught in the financial crisis and lost your savings, retirement funds, home, and/or perhaps your job, then you know all too well that our financial system played a major role in this crisis.

Despite that, changing our banking system is unthinkable. We cannot tame bankers, and we certainly cannot govern them. They are the most powerful entity in our society. So powerful, in fact, that when they crash our economy, as in the recent housing crash, we lend them more money and even ask them to manage the recovery. While we may not be able to control or change the banking system, we can attempt to fix our federal monetary system and hope that it will eventually lead to a better banking system.

What I propose for the US monetary system is not intended to address all the issues with banking or Wall Street, but to shake the system's foundation altogether, forcing a new banking system to emerge. So first let's take a quick look at how the US monetary system works.

We can define a monetary system as the way a government makes money available to its economy and manages it. In the US, the Federal Reserve (the Fed) is the most prominent player in our monetary system. The Fed is the central bank, or bankers' bank, in the US. It consists of twelve regional banks and a public Board of Governors appointed by the president and approved by the senate. The Fed is responsible for the US monetary policy, the supervision of commercial banks, and providing financial services.

According to the Federal Reserve: "Monetary policy is made by the Federal Open Market Committee (FOMC), which consists of the (five) members of the Board of

Governors of the Federal Reserve System and five Reserve Bank presidents."*

The other player in the US monetary system is the US Department of the Treasury. Unlike the Fed and commercial banks, the Treasury Department is a branch of the government and is responsible for the integrity of the US financial system. The US Mint and the Bureau of Engraving and Printing are both agencies of the Treasury Department and are responsible for coinage and printing Federal Reserve notes, respectively. A Federal Reserve note is what we know as paper money.

The process of creating new money can be simplified in the following steps: The US Treasury Department issues IOUs (I owe you) known as US Treasury securities, which have various maturity dates and include Treasury bills, notes, and bonds among others. The Fed buys these securities by printing Federal Reserve notes, and that is how new money is created.

The Fed manages the availability of money in the US economy by selling or buying Treasury securities. When the Fed buys Treasury securities already in circulation, it increases the amount of money in circulation. Conversely, when it sells them, it reduces the money in circulation. Availability of money can lead to inflation while its absence can cause deflation and potentially recession. This mechanism is a critical tool in the Fed's arsenal to manage the US economy.

The money created in this fashion is known as currency— that is what you and I think of when we talk about money. However, currency is just a fraction of the money that exists in the system. Money can also exist in the form of credit or debit, or on a balance sheet. The balance in your savings account exists in the form of a number or data and not as currency, but it is still money.

When banks were conceived, the idea was that they would issue notes or money in exchange for the collateral in their vault, namely, gold. That simply meant that if they issued a dollar, they had a dollar worth of gold in their vault. As they realized that it did not matter how much gold they had, but how much they could lend, they started lending more money than the amount they had in gold.

In this fashion, similar to the US government, banks can create money by simply lending you money. When you borrow money from the bank, you are exchanging an IOU for the money you receive. In some cases, banks are required to have a reserve of up to 10% of what they lend. When this requirement exists, a bank must have one dollar in paper money or other forms of collateral to lend ten dollars.

In the past, governments used to print money equal to the amount of gold they held in reserve. This was known as the gold standard. There was an equal amount of gold in reserve as there was money in circulation — paper money was as good as gold. The gold standard was replaced in 1971 by the current system, which is a debt-based monetary system. In the current monetary system, the US government issues treasury securities when it prints money and pays interest on these IOUs.

The issue with the debt-based monetary system is that our government not only goes into debt to create money but also pays interest on the money it prints. As a result, the system requires constant infusions of cash, leading to the devaluation of money over time. As taxpayers, we pay for the interest on the money that our government borrows, we pay the interest our banks charge while using our money, and we pay as our money loses value. According to *Forbes*, "A dollar in 1971 was worth less than 19 cents in 2012."*

I propose a conceptually simple solution: change our monetary system from debt-based to resource-based and have our government receive interest rather than pay it.

Does this solution seem outrageous? On its face, perhaps, as it will have some novel consequences; namely, there will be no Fed and the monetary policy will not be made by bankers any longer. Banks will not be allowed to lend more than the value of their assets, which would reduce the availability of capital. More importantly, there will be a one-time adjustment to the value of the dollar since it would no longer be supported by unlimited debt, but by a finite amount of our resources. All of this, of course, will be magnified and exaggerated by bankers, who will hate the change and fight it tooth and nail, and will ensure that we feel the sting of the change. Whatever the value of the dollar may become, though, it would be its real value. While these are severe consequences of changing our monetary system, on reflection, this solution is not as outlandish as it appears at first and is necessary for our country.

With the new monetary system in place, our country's resources and assets will be used as collateral for the money, similar to the way gold was used prior to the current monetary system. These collaterals encompass natural resources, which include land, water, timber, crops, oil, gas, coal, gold, and silver among others. Also included is our infrastructure: highways, bridges, railroads, etc., as well as factories, buildings, houses, and so on. Also included are foreign currencies owned by the US and foreign debts owed to the US.

Some of these resources, such as oil and gas, are exhaustible. Others, such as buildings or railroads, may be depreciable. This would not be a drawback of this resource-based system, but a constant incentive to use our natural resources cleverly, to build our country and improve our production and exports, and to maintain and build infrastructure.

Throughout history, there have been more powerful empires than the US — such as the Roman, Persian, Ottoman, and British empires — all of which have managed their finances without paying interest to conduct their affairs. It's true that some of these empires relied on taxes from their territories and on ransacking newly acquired ones to fund their finances. Nevertheless, they did not pay interest. It is, in fact, ludicrous for a superpower to pay interest on the money it prints. When it does, it becomes questionable where the power lies — with the superpower or the parties receiving the interest? To use a Thomas Jefferson's quote: "And to preserve their independence, we must not let our rulers load us with perpetual debt."*

With the government paying no interest, the banking sector will have to rely on its own resources to conduct business, and there is no shortage of resources for bankers. The top sixty-five global banks' market cap is $4.92 trillion — that is $4,922,280,000,000. The market cap for the twelve largest banks in the US is $1.32 trillion.* So with no interest paid by the US government, banks will not collapse, they will simply operate differently. With my suggested monetary system, the government will no longer lend money to the banks, but instead to the country's infrastructure.

In such a system, a committee, similar to the Board of Governors, would be appointed by Congress. It would be prudent for this committee to consist of economists and financiers, but not bankers. This committee will set the criteria for who can borrow from the government and at what rates since there will be no Federal Reserve. One or more new nonprofit entities will be formed to manage this lending. Freddie Mac and Fannie Mae may be reorganized to handle mortgages as an example of such organizations. There would be two broad categories of borrowers: individuals and corporations. For individuals, the new nonprofit organization will issue mortgages at the lowest possible rate, only high enough to cover the cost of managing these mortgages and any risk associated with them. The rates must be low, because qualified borrowers will be borrowing their own money from the government. To put this rate in perspective, the bank rate, which is the rate paid by commercial banks when borrowing, has been around 0.00–0.25%.* A new set of rules will be established to ensure that no intermediary is added to the process; otherwise, we will eventually revert to the system we have today. Mortgages will be issued to individuals only for purchasing a primary residence to encourage home ownership. Banks may offer and provide other types of mortgages, such as loans for a second property.

The government will be able to provide student loans to be repaid automatically once a student starts earning money. The automatic repayment ensures that loans are repaid. This type of loan carries low interest rates similar to the other loans we have discussed here. This will promote the pursuit of a higher education and secure the future of our country.

On the corporate level, loans may be issued to organizations involved in improving the country's infrastructure. These are organizations that manage a broad category of projects ranging from producing renewable energy to improving electrical grids, building high-speed railroads, housing, and so on. These loans would be backed by the borrowers' assets.

In our current system, the government manages the money supply and the state of the economy by shifting the interest rates and the supply of money. In the new monetary system, the government will be able to continue this practice, but only as far as it pertains to the loans it issues.

With the new monetary policy, banks will be required to lend against their assets and depositors' money (the money in your savings accounts, checking accounts, etc.). When there is a "run on the bank," banks must use their own assets to borrow from the government, just as you and I do now when we use our homes as security for mortgages.

For most of us, rallying behind a change in the US monetary policy is farfetched; yet, that is exactly what I am suggesting. We typically have difficulties with complex issues and, as a result, we avoid them. A good example is global warming. The fact that it's global and requires global efforts is scary enough without considering its underlying science. A monetary system not only shares the complexity of global warming but also has similar powerful adversaries. Oil companies like us to treat global warming as a complex matter and leave it alone the same way bankers want us to leave our monetary system alone. The difference is that our monetary system and the changes it needs don't have some theoretical effect somewhere in the world, but real effects on our wealth today. I would like to take the time here to explain some of its effects, and I hope that I can convey my point and that you demand changes.

During the recent housing collapse, banks foreclosed on properties with mortgages bearing high interest rates. Meanwhile, the government pumped money into the banks at a 0% interest rate. In 2008, Congress approved a $700 billion-dollar bailout to stabilize our financial system. When all is said and done, the actual amount, which came to light after Bloomberg won a court case against the Fed and a group of the biggest US banks, was a whopping $7.77 trillion.* Bloomberg also reported that US banks earned $13 billion in profit on the bailout loans they received from the government. Please take a moment to reflect on this.

If we allocated blame equally for the market crash in 2008, we could state that people borrowed and banks lent irresponsibly; so both banks and borrowers would be to blame. However, when the Fed intervened, banks profited by $13 billion while over 4.4 million of our homes were fore-closed upon.* The government could have simply bought these mortgages from the banks at a fair market value, which would have been a substantial discount from their origi-nal amount, and then offered them back to homeowners at a lower interest rate. This would have repaid the banks for their loans at a fair market value, which is a standard busi-ness practice, and prevented the conversion of homeowners to renters. It would also have cushioned the housing crash to more of a hard landing and prevented the wipeout of the mid-dle class. Some financially weaker banks would have gone out of business as a result, and larger banks would have become smaller and more manageable. Such a government intervention would have also been more in line with the free-market economy.

If you obtain a thirty-year mortgage for a quarter of a million dollars at a 5.5% rate to buy a home, you would pay more in interest than in principle to finance it; you would be paying around $725 a month in interest—that is $261,000 over the life of the loan. To qualify for this mortgage, you must also make $60,000, not accounting for property taxes and home insurance. Since 2008, the bank rate has been under 0.25%. If you could obtain the same mortgage at twice the bank rate, or 0.50%, you would pay a total of $19,270, or $54 a month, in interest, and you would only need to make about $32,000 to qualify. Again, please take a moment to reflect about this.

There are $1.2 trillion dollars in outstanding student loans in the US.* Even at a historic low, the average interest rate is still 4.66%, while the bank rate is 0.25%. On average, it takes students about twenty years to repay their loan.* Making the same monthly payments, but with a 0.5% interest rate, it would take almost half of the time, or about eleven years, to repay these student loans.

We do not just pay interest on mortgages, auto loans, student loans, etc.; we also pay interest in taxes. A portion of our taxes pays for the government's outstanding debt. In 2013, we paid $222.75 billion in interest.* That is over $700 for every person living in the US, or about $2,800 per family of four, just in fiscal year 2013. It is about time that we get our house in order.

This new monetary policy would be radically different

from the one the world uses today, which is the one we once asked the world to use. If we were able to change our monetary system from the gold standard to the bankers' debt-based standard before, it is within our means to change it again—this time from the bankers' standard to the people's infrastructure-and-resource-based standard.

31

The Lottery

★ ★ ★ ★

otteries take a little money from a large group of people and create one super-rich person. Since the lottery draws on the hope of becoming a millionaire, it is not surprising that the working class plays it more often than the rich. In doing so, it is a form of taxation on lower-income families. In a perfect society, we would not promote this wealth disparity; instead, we would attempt to raise the minimum standard of living for the entire society. However, it is hard to conceive of weaning states completely off this money-making mechanism, so what I envision is a slight change to the lottery that may go a long way.

Currently there is a single jackpot-winning number in each drawing for any given game. Only if there are matching tickets is the jackpot awarded. As a result, one or two people usually win these multimillion-dollar jackpots. Since I do not believe that we can eliminate the lottery, I believe we must get a better socioeconomic result by having more winners with smaller winnings, rather than the usual one or two mega-million winners. Playing a lottery game that produces tens of millionaires each time is as exciting as one that creates one mega-millionaire, and it would be much better for society. Furthermore, state governments would still make as much revenue as before.

What I recommend is that with each drawing, the system pays a net amount of one million in cash—after taxes and fees are deducted—to one or more people. As winnings would be based on a partial match, smaller winnings would also be possible as they are today. Let's assume that it takes two million dollars to pay the winner one million after taxes and fees are deducted, and that the jackpot for the week is two hundred million. In theory, the lottery would draw numbers until at least a hundred million is given away, meaning that fifty winners would win a net amount of one million in cash. The remaining amount will be added to the next week's jackpot and the game continues. A portion of money should always remain and be passed to the next drawing to ensure that there is enough money to cover any number of winners, since the number of winners and the total winnings are known only when the drawing is over.

The reason that only half of the money is given away during a drawing is that until winning numbers are drawn, lottery officials do not know how many people have won. Since there can never be more winnings than the jackpot, a reserve is necessary. Here is an example of the drawing process for a $200 million jackpot, ignoring partial winnings:

- There are 13 matches on the first set of numbers (first winning numbers drawn) and a total of $26 million in winnings thus far.
- There are 22 matches on the second drawing, or $44 million won, giving a total of $70 million in winnings.
- There are zero matches on the third set of numbers.
- There are 30 matches on the fourth set of numbers, resulting in a total of $130 million.

The drawing for the week stops since winnings have surpassed the $100 million threshold of the $200 million jackpot, and the $70 million remaining in the jackpot is passed on to the next week's game. In total, there are sixty-five winners, or sixty-five new millionaires. Instead of the jackpot amount, the number of winners will create excitement for the next game. Players will also be more engaged since there are many chances of winning. While this does not change the purpose of the game, it will produce many millionaires, rather than a few mega-millionaires.

32

Transparent Trading

★ ★ ★ ★

Our economy and every other developed economy in the world are centered on production and export, as represented by the performance of corporations—primarily companies with large market capitalization—and by our natural resources, such as oil, gas, and precious metals. The value of our money, our savings and retirement security, and even the value of our homes depend on the value of the stocks of such companies, gold, and oil, even if we personally do not own any of these assets. Typically, when the price of oil goes up, everything else goes up, since the higher price of oil translates into higher costs of transporting raw and finished goods and higher production costs. As prices go up, the value of our money goes down, since we can buy less with the same amount of money. Higher prices of goods mean less sales and revenue, and higher production costs mean smaller margins, which, in turn, lead to lower profit for companies. As investors witness their investments shrink due to the lower stock prices as well as the declining value of money (and of interest received on the money), they seek refuge in gold, increasing gold prices. In short, when all is well, gold and oil cost less, but when things are tough, gold and oil cost more.

Of course, all of this should be simply a function of supply and demand, which is a natural phenomenon — just as one can charge more for ice cream in Miami Beach than in Alaska. If oil is in short supply, or if there is not enough gold to satisfy the demand, the price of oil or gold will rise and the value of everything else will drop.

A market driven by supply and demand requires a clear understanding of the available supply and demand. In other words, if the price of an ice-cream bar is based on supply and demand, one should know the number of ice-cream bars available and estimate how many buyers there may be. Interestingly enough, no unbiased source can ever tell us with any level of certainty what the volume of gold and oil reserves are. Sources that attempt to estimate these volumes have every incentive to manipulate the market. There is simply no reliable way to estimate the available supply of the two assets on which our economy depends most heavily. We do not know exactly how much oil lies below the ground or how easily Saudi Arabia can drastically reduce its output due to a peculiar terrorist attack, or how much gold sits in Swiss banks or in the basements of palaces in oil-rich countries.

The problem, though, is not so much the supply of and demand for gold or oil, but the system of managing the trading of these commodities. If the trading, the supply of gold, or the flow of oil can be controlled, then our economy and money can be manipulated.

The prices of oil and other commodities are not just affected by supply and demand, but also by promises of future transactions, commonly called futures. Futures contracts are agreements to a trade on a set date in the future based on a price agreed upon today. Even if you are familiar with futures, take a moment to think about it. While futures are simply investment tools, can you think of any smarter way to manipulate the market? Aren't futures on a large scale a self-fulfilling prophecy? The oil stocks automatically open higher—as they should—when the futures of oil are higher. In plain English, the price of oil goes up even though there is currently no change in supply or demand.

Imagine those who manage portfolios worth hundreds of billions of dollars and the level of control they have over the market; yet you and I participate in this game and bet our children's future on it.

The larger issue revolving around trading is the lack of transparency in trading systems and ownership. If you owned billions of dollars in shares of various corporations, you would hire mathematicians, physicists, and other experts to build sophisticated models that can be triggered by computers to manipulate the market, and you would use them to manage your transactions. Well, companies do exactly that. This algorithmic trading is known as black-box trading, and was responsible for about one third of all trading in the US in 2010.* In 2009, Goldman Sachs filed charges against one of its former employees accusing him of stealing its rapid-fire stock-and-commodities-trading software that could be used to manipulate the market.* These charges prove that bankers, or at least Goldman Sachs, have software capable of market manipulation.

When we trade or invest in stocks in the short term, we may lose or gain. In the long term, however, we are simply playing a game of musical chairs with nine chairs and ten players. In this analogy, seven of the players are permanently sitting and any of them can stop the music. The other three players represent our holdings—our savings, retirement accounts, our children's futures, and so on. The seven sitting players are market makers and manipulators, and when they stop the music, we lose. Sometimes we lose our homes, sometimes our savings, sometimes our retirement and our quality of life; inevitably, we always lose.

We have talked about other steps to correct our financial system in other chapters. Here, we need to address transparency in trading and ownership. We must demand that information about stockholders of public companies be not just public but readily available online when they own above a certain percentage of shares, perhaps more than one hundredth of a percent. While this alone will not change the musical chairs game, it will give us enough insight to engage in the game more cautiously. If this requirement goes into effect, the trading conducted by such shareholders becomes transparent, since a trade is a transfer of ownership. With more transparency in trading, the incidence of black-box trading would be drastically reduced and so would our risks in owning stocks.

While I do not mean to discourage investing, I would recommend that before considering any investment, you pay your debts and mortgage first. The need to pay your debt and mortgage is certain, but the return on your investments is not guaranteed. Transparency in trading would make investment less risky.

33

Energy and Oil

★ ★ ★ ★

I f someone discovered a method to deliver free, unlimited, usable energy, would it become public knowledge, or would it be kept a secret? That is an interesting question. If I asked you to name one thing on earth on which our survival depends, you might correctly answer air, water, or food, but my answer would be energy. We think of money as the most tradable commodity; while that is correct in economic terms, in terms of real-world exchanges, the easiest thing to "trade" is energy. Using energy, we can easily produce clean air, fresh water, and more crops than we desire. Energy builds our economies and converts raw material into finished goods for our consumption, industries, and military. It is said that if you control money, you control the world. I would say instead: control energy and you control the world.

The world acquires about 82% of its energy from fossil fuels (31.4% from oil, 21.3% from gas, and 29% from coal), 10% from biofuel and waste, 2.4% from hydroelectric power,

4.8% from nuclear power, and 1% from other sources.* Hydroelectric plants use earth's natural cycle and, as such, are the cleanest means of energy production (notwithstanding the destruction of farmland to build dams). Unfortunately, the type of water used to produce this energy is limited, even without considering global warming. Fossil fuels unleash stored energy in the form of carbon that has been stored over millions of years, adding it back to the atmosphere. As such, they pollute the air and increase its temperature. They are also limited in amount, even though no one can tell us with any level of certainty just how limited the supply is. Oil, the most popular of all fossil fuels, happens to be concentrated in a few regions of the world, making these regions unstable.

We get about 6% of our energy from nuclear and renewable sources. Nuclear and solar energy have more in common than we think; both are available in abundance and both are actually nuclear in nature. Of course, we are not too concerned about the nuclear reactions taking place in the sun and just enjoy its bright light. On the other hand, the nuclear energy produced here on Earth creates waste for us to deal with. Our reliance on fossil fuels subjects us to manipulation, and the cost of a gallon of gasoline goes way beyond the few dollars that we pay at the pump. We have to turn over a new leaf and make changes beyond campaign promises. We need real changes! Switching our gasoline cars to electric vehicles is nice, but not a real change. Most of our electricity is still being produced by fossil energy, so the end result is the same. Electric cars are a step in the right direction. If we manage to get most of our energy from the sun, nuclear, or chemical reactions, our cars need to be electric to take advantage of it.

We have written off nuclear power plants for safety reasons. Both traditional nuclear fission and newer nuclear fusion are great sources of energy that we do not have to wage war for, and that are immensely safer than they were a few decades ago. Still, a nuclear power plant disaster every twenty to thirty years makes the safety issues hard to ignore, even though the failures are regulatory and not technological. With Fukushima, Japan, fresh in everyone's mind, overcoming this concern may prove to be difficult. Nevertheless, we have to keep our minds open and consider new options.

The sun is another source of energy that will not go away any time soon — and when it does, we will no longer be here to need energy. The beauty of solar energy is that it's not only clean and abundant, but also available everywhere. Unlike other traditional sources of electricity, which have to be produced in one place and distributed, the energy from the sun can be harvested wherever it's needed. Why not change every surface to one that converts sunlight into energy whenever possible? We can keep our roof shingles, sidings, houses, and buildings mostly looking as they do now, but with materials that harvest energy from the sun and generate electricity. That's attainable today. Where there is a will, there is a way.

If we do not do enough to promote solar energy, we should at least not discourage it. Some power companies add a surcharge when subscribers use solar power as their main source of electricity. Such companies claim that the surcharge is to pay for their infrastructure. Whether that claim is entirely true or such fees are to discourage people from using solar power, the result is the same: it discourages people from using solar power. We should pass laws to stop such surcharges.

With gas prices falling as I write, we may become short-sighted and forget that a war across the globe can skyrocket oil prices and send our economy into a recession. We must demand a better and cheaper source of energy from our government so that we can end our dependency on oil, power up our economy for generations to come, and protect our planet.*

34

Post Office

★ ★ ★ ★

There was a time when we rushed to greet the mailman and find a letter from Grandma or a postcard from a faraway cousin, along with our utility bills. The US mail, or more accurately the US Postal Service (USPS), has played a major role in US history primarily as a means of communications. A postcard that shows up in our mailbox is part of a complex system consisting of advanced technologies and a dedicated workforce. According to the USPS, the system generated over $67 billion in gross revenue in 2013, employed 489,727 people, delivered over 158 billion pieces of mail, and lost $5 billion.*

It is an inescapable reality that the Postal Service's core business of communication has been disappearing in its current format and that, while it offers many services to maintain its infrastructure, it is not sustainable in its current format. In addition to that, the USPS's first-class mail service, which is its flagship feature, promotes inefficiencies throughout our society. At some point, first-class mail was the main vehicle for the delivery of correspondences and bills, but it is no longer so. In 2013, first-class mail accounted for only 13% of all USPS deliveries by revenue.* Each day, like most Americans, I receive a half dozen to a dozen pieces of mail. I spend a few minutes looking through them and opening items that seem to be important, but most are not. I get magazines primarily because their publishers refuse to provide them in digital format only. Half of the mail I receive is brochures, ads, pamphlets, and other junk mail that I do not need or want. Almost all my first-class mail consists of offers, both legitimate and fraudulent. After I dispose of generic materials and shred those items containing my personal information, I end up with a few legitimate pieces of mail, which I shred after scanning and electronically storing them.

If I were to convey that process to a visitor from Mars, it would go like this:

Me: There are some entities that want to tell me about their new product or to send me a receipt for the product that I have bought from them, or the agreement I've reached with them, and so on. What they want to send or tell me is already stored in their systems in digital format. To get this to me, they use printers and convert these digital copies to paper copies. To do so, they use time, electricity, ink, and paper.

Martian: What is paper?

Me: Paper used to be a tree, which is this precious living resource that takes the poisonous CO_2 out of our atmosphere and produces oxygen so that we can breathe and live. So paper was a tree that has been chopped down and washed and is processed by using lots of water, chemicals, and energy while producing harmful and toxic pollution.

Martian: So you chop down what is critical to your survival so you can have paper?

Me: Yes. In that way, we are in fact funny creatures. We also grow crops to fuel our vehicles, while over a billion of us do not have enough food. Anyway . . . so they take the digital stuff, print it, and send it to us.

Martian: So it must be easy and efficient to send the paper around, right?

Me: Not at all. To do so, there are over 600,000 people using over 200,000 vehicles.

Martian: Is that a lot?

Me: That's the largest fleet in the world, well, at least on earth, and it uses gasoline-powered engines mostly.

Martian: Well, I assume that there is no other way to deliver this stuff that you must have. What do you do with it when you get it?

Me: Some goes straight into the trash because it's neither important nor recyclable! Some will be read and then put away, in a pile that will be trashed later. People like me scan the rest to convert it to a digital format, then shred and discard it. In the best-case scenario, some of this material gets recycled using more resources.

Martian: You convert digital documents into hard copy using tons of precious resources to produce and deliver it, only for it to end up in landfills in one way or another, and if any is important, you convert it back to digital format? I do not get it.

Me: I do not get it, either.

The post office has to change. Although the postal workers' union may not agree with the changes that I suggest, just like any other union, it needs to face today's realities. If we do what's right while we still have options, we can control the change. In doing so, we can reposition workers who otherwise could find themselves without jobs.

I suggest phasing in the following changes:

- The Postal Service should get out of parcel delivery by selling its services to a private company and transferring some of its employees as part of the deal.
- It should replace its six days of delivery with once-a-week delivery. Different neighborhoods would have an established delivery day, just as trash collection is done today. This could be phased out over a ten-year period.
- It should close all of its customer walk-in facilities, but maintain facilities for sorting, distribution, and digital services.

- It should be required to use electric cars so that, in ten years, its entire fleet would be electric.

These changes would have no substantial effect other than forcing our entire society to stop the waste and embrace the digital age. In a ten-year period, these changes would reduce the number of postal workers to somewhere between 100,000 and 200,000 and the number of vehicles to under 50,000. The economic and environmental impact would be greater than that of any other single change that I have proposed.

I also suggest the following changes now to set the stage for the changes suggested above:

- The USPS should provide email addresses for individuals as Google and Yahoo do, such as someone@usps.com. These would be our official email addresses. These accounts will be set up so that they can be used only by the USPS. We cannot use our USPS email to send an email out. Internet Service Providers (ISPs) would be set up so that they would not be able to route USPS emails unless they were generated by the USPS. The misuse of these email addresses should be declared a felony as it is with the mail today. These steps would eliminate fraud and abuse of official email.
- It should create a portal for each user so that the USPS can link physical addresses to email addresses with the USPS domain. The USPS would control any changes just as it handles changes of physical addresses today.
- The portal would allow its users to select what type of

mail they want to receive and whether they want to receive it via email or in hard copy.

- It should provide recipients an option to receive mail electronically. When recipients receive their mail electronically, senders pay a small fee and recipients pay nothing. When recipients choose the hardcopy format, as they do today, senders will pay fees similar to what they pay for stamps today, and recipients will also pay a small fee.

- With this option we could choose, for example, to receive regular mail from individuals, but digitized mail from others such as banks. We could also create a list of senders whose mail we would like to receive via hard copy. This way we would have the option to receive junk mail for a fee or receive its free digital version. Additionally, we should be able to choose what categories of junk mail we want to receive and in what format.

When these changes are in place, the USPS could require senders to provide an electronic copy of items being mailed as well as a hard copy, when a hard copy exists. It could charge advertisers differently for delivering their ads depending on whether they are in electronic or hard copy formats. Since the USPS costumers select these options actively, this service is highly valuable to advertisers. For example, if I indicate that I am not interested in sports, companies that sell sporting goods would not waste money sending me ads. Since the new system would save advertisers money, it should be easy to implement. Eventually the USPS would have plug-ins (API) for companies to use. These plug-ins would interact with various companies' mail systems and facilitate delivery without any other touch points. Since the USPS is the official vehicle of mail delivery, its email system would become the official USPS delivery system.

The post office could eventually offer print-on-demand services similar to what companies like Amazon offer today. With this option, businesses will send only digital copies of their materials to the USPS and pay only for the number of hardcopies printed as determined by the recipients. In this fashion, not a single household will receive a hardcopy brochure unless it has asked for it. For example, if I am an auto enthusiast, I would indicate my interest in automotive goods. Furthermore, I would indicate whether I would like to receive materials in electronic or digital copy. When businesses serving the auto industry send out marketing brochures, the USPS knows that I would like to receive them and whether to send them in a digital or hard-copy format. This is the ultimate in supply-chain efficiencies.

35

National Health and Biometric Database

★ ★ ★ ★

Most of us are concerned, if not afraid, about the amount of our personal information that is being stored, how it may be used, and who may access it. Google may know more about some of us than our families do, but Google is like a scoop of Haagen-Dazs ice cream: it's impossible to resist. Of course, if Google has it, our government has it.

This is the information age. We are generating more data than ever before, and as it becomes easier to collect and store data, there will be even more data. As we develop more data, we also find smarter ways to analyze and understand it. The new technologies in sensors, batteries, and communications will allow us to collect physical and mental feedback from our body, learn about it, and act on it. We are not just talking about shopping habits, but our hormone levels and our dreams.

Yes, the information about us may be misused, but the availability of new data is inevitable—it will be generated and stored whether we like it or not. Second, the benefit that comes from this data is much greater than any potential abuse. We do need to ensure that the information is used properly, and we need to embrace it and welcome it. I believe that a National Health and Biometric Database (NHBD) should be formed, under the oversight of a new nonprofit organization. This organization will be responsible for gathering, storing, and releasing the information gathered.

In the past, the information available on an individual was limited and stored in unrelated databases for various purposes, and not necessarily for healthcare. For example, we considered the frequency and intensity of a headache, our blood pressure, and pulse a part of our medical record. However, our behaviors, such as the length of time we spend at a computer or on social sites each day or whether we use a wireless phone handset or a speaker phone were considered a part of social data, and, of course, this information would only have been collected for a study. And information on our DNA did not even exist. Now these databases are no longer necessarily distinct, and it would not be smart to keep them that way. Do we get headaches because of our genetic makeup, the amount of time we spend at a computer, lack of sleep, or changes in the weather? Wearables (wearable technology) are in their infancy and already produce tons of data on us. Connecting these various data points produces conclusions that otherwise would be impossible to reach.

Currently, health insurance companies collect and store data on us, but we do not benefit from this data. The same is done by hospitals, pharmacies, and physicians, yet we see only limited benefits from their data collection. We should stop all organizations from maintaining any data with regards to our health and biometrics, including DNA information, and assign such a task to the NHBD exclusively. These entities, including our physicians, hospitals, labs, etc., would be able to collect, access, and update our data, but would not maintain them. If the NHBD has the task of collecting and maintaining data, it will create efficiencies throughout the health system, remove our personal data from the hands of private organizations, and allow us to manage the data in almost the same way as we manage our credit information. The NHBD will not only reduce potential abuse of our information, but also turn our data into a powerful tool for us.

Again, you may be thinking that such a measure would allow the government to access our data, but the government, insurance companies, service providers, as well as any other caregivers or payers of your medical bills already have legal access to our data.* So, as it is, the entities that we may be concerned about already have access to our information, but we do not benefit from the upside and efficiency of such data collection. The NHBD will change that.

36

Genetic Discrimination Bill

★ ★ ★ ★

We cannot stop shedding information. We generate information as we talk, eat, look, breathe, and even think and dream. In fact, we even produce information by doing nothing. Most of the information generated must be stored to be of any use, or shared and cross-referenced in order to be valuable. Ample data on us exists, whether we like it or not. Our concern should be how this data is used, or more specifically, if it is being used against us. I believe that we need a new bill to bar discrimination against us based on our biometrics, and our DNA in particular.

The National Health and Biometric Database can play a critical role in managing our health information, but our genetic data could also be used as a basis to qualify for employment. The Genetic Information Nondiscrimination Act of 2008 (GINA) already protects us against such discrimination in employment as well as in health insurance. However, this act should be expanded to include protection against the use of genetic data as a basis for school admissions so that all people are evaluated on their initiative, willingness, and experience, and not on their DNA.

37

SAM

★ ★ ★ ★

In the next chapter, we will discuss National Healthcare System or NHS. The NHS would rely on a robust software program that would use workflow automation to manage its components. To understand how this workflow works, think of your car navigation system. You set your destination and it takes you there. In doing so, it already knows your current location, and it knows the city map, including streets and highways, their speed limits, restrictions, traffic conditions, exceptional situations such as road closures, etc. The navigation system combines this information and uses its logic to get you to your destination. Workflow automation works somewhat the same way and has been used by corporations for over twenty years.

I refer to this system of hardware and software as the National Healthcare System Automation Manager (NHSAM, or SAM for short). SAM would be highly robust, flexible, and intelligent, deriving its intelligence from multiple databases.

The first of these would be a medical knowledge base containing a medical dictionary, diseases and their symptoms, as well as potential treatments, all medications, their side effects and more, using the Centers for Disease Control and Prevention (CDC), the National Institutes of Health (NIH), and other sources.

Another database would be the list of healthcare providers including hospitals, labs, physicians, their services, and all other related information. To understand you and your needs, SAM would access your records from the NHBD. Finally, SAM would use the Internet for anything else that may be related to our health, such as environmental factors in a specific geographic area, pollution, humidity, temperature, etc.

Each database would have a portal, a user-facing web page or app, to allow user interaction. Various databases would enjoy various levels of openness or restriction depending on their purpose. For example, you and only people you authorized could access your NHBD to the extent necessary.

We would interact with SAM through browsers, apps, phones, and new gadgets—think of it as a combination of Amazon's customer service and Apple's Siri.* Let's say that you have a headache. You tell SAM that you have a headache. SAM considers your health records including previous instances of headaches, complaints, allergies, etc., and may ask you a series of questions to understand your symptoms. Then, SAM may suggest an over-the-counter medication. SAM, of course, can also set up an appointment for a phone consultation, a video chat with a physician, or an office visit with your healthcare providers.

SAM can also follow up with you on your headache, remind you to take your medications, arrange with your healthcare providers for follow-up, refill your prescriptions, notify your emergency contacts, and much more. Every time you interact with SAM, it learns more about you and becomes more effective.

Those of you who are not up to speed with the latest information technology and its role in our lives may think, at this point, that I am writing a sci-fi novel. I assure you that everything that I am describing here already exists and is being used in one shape or another; so let's turn our attention to technology for a few minutes.

Let's start with Watson. IBM describes Watson this way: "As a cognitive technology, Watson is a natural extension of what humans can do at their best."* If you are not familiar with Watson, I highly recommend following this link and watching a couple of videos available on the main page.*

The cognitive computing technology of Watson allows it to analyze, understand, learn, and recommend. In this manner, Watson has been learning about cancer, specifically lung cancer, similar to the way an intern learns. The joint venture of IBM, WellPoint, and Memorial Sloan Kettering Cancer Center (MSK) has allowed Watson to ingest more than 600,000 pieces of medical evidence as well as two million pages of text from forty-two medical journals and clinical trials. MSK staff and nurses have spent over 14,700 hours in hands-on training with Watson, sharing their experience and expertise in treating hundreds of thousands of cancer patients. As a result, Watson can sift through 1.5 million patients' records, their history, their treatments and outcomes, and provide physicians treatment options in a matter of seconds.*

On another front, global medical wearables, a $2.9 billion market in 2014, will grow to $8.3 billion in revenue by 2019.* As the name implies, medical wearables are devices that we wear to sense and/or interact with our body. Most wearables today are sensors, but as technology improves we will see more wearables that not only sense but address a problem. Wearables currently cover a broad range of activities, including monitoring our heart rate, temperature, perspiration, brainwaves, and blood oxygen. Technologically enhanced diapers can even sense infection and dehydration.*

The availability and speed of the Internet has opened another front with what's known as the "Internet of things," which simply refers to the interconnection of various devices through the Internet. The Internet of things simply allows one device to communicate with another device. For example, your home security can detect that you are not home and communicate with your thermostat to lower the temperature, whereas your car might communicate to your house that you're nearby, prompting the heat to go up.

Last but not least, advancements in genetics, robotics, information, and nanotechnology (GRIN) will change the way we view our health, the way we diagnose diseases, what we consider treatable, and finally the way we treat diseases. According to an estimate, it would take 160 hours a week for a doctor to keep up with these advancements, leaving him 8 hours for everything else-clearly an impossible feat for any physician.* With medical data doubling every five years, it is easy to see why technologies like Watson will be critical to the quality as well as the cost of healthcare.

In short, we have everything we need to put SAM to work. When we do, the technology would change the way in which we view healthcare since it would be used on a national scale. SAM would be capable of detecting and analyzing patterns such as a flu outbreak and notifying authorities much faster and far more efficiently than is now possible. Authorities such as the CDC could then establish a treatment plan for the outbreak through SAM, which would instantly notify all parties involved.

SAM would track not only the spread of the disease but also the effectiveness of the treatment or the vaccination. SAM could take factors into consideration that are difficult, if not impossible, to assess today. For instance, it could find correlations between a vaccine and race, climate, sex, age, or medications. SAM could prevent an epidemic or help to locate patient zero, the individual who starts an epidemic. It could be used as a tool to help us understand the various environmental factors that cause or help prevent diseases such as cancer.

Finally, SAM would serve as a powerful tool to fight biological terrorism or to deal with the aftermath of a natural disaster, not only by detecting an outbreak early, but also by anticipating a need and putting the necessary response teams on alert.

Healthcare providers would use SAM to set up their treatment plans. SAM would also be in a good position to detect conflicting treatments and drug interactions. Both you and your healthcare provider would see the entire flow or course of actions from the initial visit to the last step planned or taken. If you use a set of medical wearables, SAM can keep track of your body temperature, weight, blood pressure, glucose level, and even sleeping patterns.

As capable as SAM may be, SAM would not treat you, at least not until it is proven to be effective and we become comfortable with it. It would only facilitate your treatment, enabling better and more efficient care. Think of SAM as a personal concierge.

38

National Healthcare System

★ ★ ★ ★

I propose a National Healthcare System (NHS) that will be available to all US citizens and permanent residents. The NHS will replace Medicare and Medicaid and will be paid for with a percentage of our gross income, similar to how Medicare and Medicaid are funded today. The NHS will overhaul our healthcare system, eliminate waste, improve our quality of life, and lower the total cost of healthcare.

Before outlining the NHS, I would like to differentiate between healthcare and health insurance. Healthcare refers to any activity that supports one's health; health insurance is a policy that grants access to healthcare. The policy allows its holder to access healthcare in exchange for premiums and copayments that, in total, equal the sum of three items: the cost of the healthcare, the cost of the insurance companies' overhead, and the profit of insurance companies' shareholders.

Before Obamacare, there were 48 million uninsured people in America.* Obamacare requires anyone who is not insured to subscribe to a health insurance plan. I believe that in a democratic society everyone must have access to healthcare and that healthcare should not be a privilege reserved for just a segment of society; as such, Obamacare is a step in the right direction. However, healthcare and health insurance are not the same thing. Obamacare, or the Affordable Care Act, forces Americans to access healthcare by subscribing to the services of for-profit health insurance companies.

Let's look at the act from a business perspective. An insurance company's cost of acquiring a customer should range between $100 and $1,000; that simply means that an insurance company spends an average $100 to $1,000 in marketing for every customer it acquires. The range is wide because it varies from one company to another, by region, and by the type of customer acquired. This means that Obamacare, with this single act, which forces us to acquire insurance, has saved these companies between $4.8 billion and $480 billion in marketing. This amount may be incidental to the people responsible for passing the law, but it is a significant savings for the insurance companies. In 2014, 6.8 million enrolled in a plan through healthcare.gov, Obamacare's official website.* This number does not include the 850,000 enrolling through state marketplaces. On one hand, this is 7.65 million people who did not have health coverage before; on the other hand, that translates to around $38.25 billion in revenues for health insurance companies.*

Obamacare enforces its requirement by penalizing companies that do not offer coverage and individuals who do not obtain coverage. Companies of certain sizes will pay a penalty of $2,000 per employee without coverage or with inadequate coverage.* Individuals without coverage pay a penalty of an average of $331 per person or $637 per family depending on their income.* The Supreme Court has recognized this penalty as taxes and, as such, it is a legal practice.* While the federal government can levy reasonable taxes and the penalties could be considered a form of taxation, the Affordable Care Act itself forces us to pay for the services of private companies. The need for national healthcare is the justification for Obamacare's mandatory health insurance. To draw an analogy here, this law is like saying that since every citizen needs drinking water, the government, rather than ensuring that we all have drinking water, will penalize us if we do not buy a bottle of water every day. I find the Supreme Court ruling disappointing and believe that it has paved the way for new forms of abuse by large corporations under the pretense of protecting us.

Additional problems with the mandatory health insurance involve Medicare. Granted that we all need healthcare, let's assume that we should get it through health insurance coverage. In general, the younger working segment of the population is the healthiest and requires the least care, while the older segment requires the most care; consequently, the younger population costs the system less than older people. Common sense dictates that we should cover everyone under a single system, such as the NHS, to offset the cost and average it out, but that is not how it has been done. Taxpayers have been asked to bear the cost of insuring the elderly in the form of Medicare and to pay the cost of their own healthcare by obtaining private health insurance.

Prior to Obamacare, this system may have been justified, since one was not required to have health insurance and coverage was voluntary. With Obamacare, we directly pay the cost of healthcare for the elderly, as we should, and then we pay for our own care by subscribing to health insurance, whose premiums contribute to the handsome profits of private corporations. With Obamacare, our nation has come the closest it has ever been to having national health care, but the system has been built on a faulty foundation. The entire system needs to be overhauled and rebuilt on solid ground so that all Americans may enjoy national healthcare.

Before we explore my proposed National Healthcare System, I would also like to discuss a current trend, namely the consolidation of physicians. Doctors join a big cluster of physicians not necessarily by choice, but because it is increasingly difficult for an independent physician to compete with large corporations that offer the same services. This simply means that soon it will be difficult to find an independent physician.

As more doctors are consolidated into large groups of doctors, the personal choice in health care will be reduced and the prices will potentially go up. Until recently, paying for a doctor's visit meant that we paid a doctor for his (or her) costs and his time. With consolidated practices comes corporate overhead, which can get paid for by the savings created in the areas of administration and billing. However, prices may ultimately go up due to the absence of competitors and lack of government oversight. Additionally, in this system, a physician's performance is subject to corporate productivity metrics, which place the revenues generated by physicians alongside the quality of service rendered, patient satisfaction, and other evaluative factors. That is how other professional corporations such as law firms and accounting services have operated for years. These metrics lead to physicians spending less time with their patients and becoming less personable.

The consolidation of physicians limits the options for those with modest means, that is, the majority of the population. So while it is nice to have options, when it comes to healthcare, options become a luxury that we cannot afford regardless of whether the NHS is implemented or not.

A prerequisite for my proposed NHS is a national health records database. Earlier I proposed the creation of a National Health and Biometric Database (NHBD). Use of this database would be required for every healthcare provider, and the database would maintain records of our healthcare-related activities so as to eliminate redundant tests, doctor visits, and procedures, and enable faster and more accurate diagnosis. The NHBD would maintain a digital record of our health history from cradle to grave. Through the NHBD, we could manage which providers can have access to our records, for what period of time, and to what extent, even though most of the tasks will be automated. For example, we may allow a radiologist to have one-time access, whereas our family physician would have access until we stop seeing him or her. The particular need determines the level of access, such as access to our personal information, psychological data, biometric and DNA information, or general health records. For instance, a phlebotomist would only have access to the tests ordered and not to any other information.

To protect our health data and to prevent abuse of the

database, I have also proposed a genetic discrimination bill, as discussed in an earlier chapter.

Currently companies specializing in electronic medical records (EMRs) or electronic health records (EHRs) help healthcare providers to digitize patient records and reduce paperwork, but unless the program is centralized, we would not see the full benefits of such digitization. The NHBD and the way it will be engaged by the NHS will eliminate waste, make information available where and when it is needed, and increase the efficiency of the entire system by making every patient's history available to all healthcare providers.

This may be a good time to acknowledge that, in general, the quality of our health care is among the highest in the world. We have top-flight physicians, qualified and dedicated nursing professionals, and an abundance of healthcare equipment, facilities, and infrastructure. So the issue is not the healthcare itself, but its cost. It is critical, however, to point out that the quality of healthcare may not matter if one cannot afford it.

When it comes to paying for healthcare, philosophically, we can place most people into two categories: first, people who believe that everyone should have equal access to healthcare, as I do. And second, those who believe that there should be no free lunch, and if one cannot afford it, one should not have it. Both beliefs have logical foundations. The truth is that we pay for those without healthcare, and the cost should be lower when the healthcare is not accessed through ER. So we may as well have a solid offering for everyone.

The NHS would have to rely on existing resources.

Initially, it would reach agreements with private healthcare providers such as hospitals, labs, physician groups, and others, similar to how Medicare operates today. The NHS would pay these providers as they render services. As the NHS gets established, it could develop its own facilities to have better control of its services. The best facility might be a hybrid of which the NHS would own 51% and private companies would own the remaining 49%. This arrangement would ensure a link between private and public providers.

The NHS and healthcare facilities would negotiate and set the rates for various services. Such rates would be set in such a way as to generate reasonable profits for these healthcare facilities. These rates affect the cost of healthcare, but they do not directly affect the patients or the copay amount.

The NHS would be available to all US citizens and legal residents, and we would pay its cost through taxes in the same fashion as Medicare is funded today. To access healthcare through the NHS, patients would make a copayment as they do today based on their insurance plan. The copayment would be a minimum amount that would vary slightly depending on the service rendered. The total of all copayments collected annually would make up any deficit in the NHS as the result of insufficient taxes collected. In addition, the copayments would allow occasional users of services to pay less than frequent users.

The copays might range between five dollars for prescription drugs or a physician's visit and five hundred dollars for a heart surgery. The copay must never be high enough to prevent a person from seeking care; so these amounts need to be adjusted as necessary. There may be a maximum copay per person per year to cap medical expenses and keep them affordable. The NHS would cover all healthcare-related issues including dental and vision care. There should not be any copay for screening, preventive measures, vaccines, or anything that applies to a large portion of the population and can prevent minor issues from becoming big ones.

Alternatively, copays could also be managed through a point system. In this system, points are assigned to various services. In our example, a physician's fee would be counted as five points and a major surgery as five hundred points. Healthcare providers would be paid by the NHS; therefore, when we make a copayment to a care provider, the provider has to either send the copayment to the NHS or apply it toward the amount owed to the provider by the NHS. Either way, the system would suffer from the same issues facing Medicare today: fraud and waste.

To avoid that, with the point system, there would be no monetary exchange between the patient and the healthcare provider. Instead, the NHS would report the points used by the taxpayer annually. Whether using the current copay system or the point system, the copays could be collected annually as taxes. When filing a tax return, the subscriber would provide the NHS statement as part of his or her tax records. The total in the statement would be added in as taxes owed. This will eliminate the patient billing system.

Upon check-in at a healthcare provider, patients would present any government ID that proves their citizenship or residency, and the provider would validate their eligibility. This would remove another entire, expensive layer from the healthcare system for which, at the end of the day, we taxpayers would otherwise have to pay.

In addition to reducing costs and the potential for fraud, the point system offers another benefit. Since the copayments would make up any deficit in the NHS, they would vary from one year to another and may be zero at the end of the year if there is no deficit. With the point system, the deficit can be divided by the total points used by taxpayers for the year to determine the value of a point. With the point system, we would pay only what's needed, if anything.

Whether we use traditional copayments or the point system, the NHS might allow a certain exemption for each person in each calendar year, such as 100 points. Let's call this exemption Annual Copay Exemption. As an example, let's consider a copay maximum of 200 points and copay exemption of 100 points. An individual with 75 points at the end of the year will pay nothing. Someone with 180 points at the end of the year will pay 80 points (180-100). Someone with 250 points pays 100 since the maximum is 200 points (200-100). This will encourage people to keep the use of healthcare in check, yet it will also make it affordable for those with chronic conditions or those in need of a major treatment. Such conditions should not wipe out a family's life savings.

In the previous chapter, we discussed the National Healthcare System Automated Manager or SAM. Earlier we talked about the NHS statement, which outlines our copayments for year-end tax purposes, whether in points or dollars. As you most likely have guessed, SAM would provide you with this statement without any cost to the system and in real time. Since the activities would be transparent to all parties involved, fraud and waste could be eliminated. If a root canal is performed, you would see it in your online statement, your dentist would see it in his or her activity report, and that is how the NHS would reimburse the dentist for performing the root canal. As always, transparency and simplicity leave no room for misconduct.

With the NHS, we will inevitably end up with two tiers of healthcare: one that is public and free (paid through taxes) and a second that is private and expensive. This means that physicians would have the choice to work for the NHS or for private practices once they graduate. The NHS would sponsor internships much as Medicare does today.* So in this manner, all physicians would become familiar with the NHS even if they choose to enter a private practice.

Additionally, to keep the NHS and the private sector working together, and to ensure that top doctors are available to the NHS, physicians who choose to go into a private practice would have two options: to work exclusively for the NHS for a few years before going into a private practice, or starting at a private practice. Those who start off with the NHS could spend fewer hours in the NHS in subsequent years.

The implementation of the NHS would remove the role of insurance companies as middlemen between us and healthcare providers. Health insurance is a private industry that earned $884 billion in revenues in 2013.* While a good portion of this figure was used to pay for the cost of healthcare, removing health insurance companies as middlemen eliminates their costs and their profit from the total healthcare cost. Since no employee of a health insurance company looks at your x-ray, provides you with a diagnosis, writes a prescription, or renders any service that can be considered healthcare, its elimination will be the ultimate savings for taxpayers.

With the NHS available to all citizens, health insurance companies would have to come up with exotic products to cater to the rich. An exception would apply to those health insurance companies that own and operate healthcare facilities. These companies would be prime candidates as starting points or seeds for the NHS.

Since the NHS would cover any and all healthcare-related issues from cradle to grave, it has no incentive to delay a treatment or to allow a condition to become critical. At this point, those of you familiar with universal healthcare in countries like Canada may be thinking that treatment may be delayed due to supply and demand. A delay may not be the result of supply and demand, but of inadequate infrastructure. Unlike existing universal healthcare systems, NHS combines our nations' top healthcare providers with the latest technology available including NHBD and SAM. The proposed NHS will be a model for the rest of the world. With the NHS, everyone will be entitled and encouraged to have periodic checkups and screening tests as determined by the Freedom Watch group (discussed earlier) or the American Medical Association. A committee within the Freedom Watch group consisting entirely of physicians and free from any conflict of interest would be available to make such determinations.

My last proposed step for the NHS is the elimination of healthcare-related lawsuits with the exception of pharmaceutical companies and medical equipment manufacturers. Under the NHS, no one could be sued, thus removing from the system the cost of malpractice insurance, the cost of lawyers and legal fees, unnecessary tests and treatments due to fear of lawsuits, and much bureaucracy. Most often people argue that this approach allows healthcare providers "to get away with murder," but let's bear in mind that the justice system would still be in place for cases of gross negligence and malpractice. In addition, SAM would allow us to see clearly who was involved in any activity that led to malpractice.

To implement the NHS, we have created the National Health and Biometric Database (NHBD), eliminated health insurance companies as middlemen, set lower rates with healthcare providers through agreements, eliminated the billing system, created a point system to manage copayments, absorbed Medicare and Medicaid into the NHS, and paid for the NHS through taxes. We also eliminated healthcare related law suits and created SAM, which was discussed in the previous chapter.

Let's compare Obamacare and the NHS. As taxpayers, we ultimately pay for either system. Under Obamacare, we pay for Medicare and Medicaid through taxes, and we pay private insurance premiums as well as copays and out-of-pocket deductibles. In doing so, we pay not only for healthcare but also for health insurance companies' operating costs and profits, billing costs, the cost of lawsuits, and the waste in the system. Under the NHS, we pay only for healthcare through taxes (as we do today for Medicare and Medicaid) and possibly copayments. Obamacare does not take any steps to improve healthcare or to eliminate waste or fraud; the NHS provides the next generation of health care, stops systematic fraud, reduces costs, and greatly improves services.

When we implement the NHS, we will not only have access to the next century's healthcare system, we'll also create a multi-billion-dollar market by licensing SAM to other countries and helping them bring their healthcare system to the twenty-first century. We will create a healthcare model that every country needs and wants. In addressing their needs, we will do well while we do good!

39

The War on ~~Drugs~~ Cancer

★ ★ ★ ★

Since the Revolutionary War in 1775, we've been in some sort of war once every six to seven years. Since most wars and conflicts have lasted more than a year, we've had fifty-six years free of wars in the last 240 years and fifteen years without wars in the last hundred years. The last time when we were not involved in a conflict was 1979.* We go to war sometimes to defend our freedom and our way of life; sometimes to defend others' freedom and way of life. Going to war perhaps goes with the territory of being a superpower. As of this writing, we are involved in conflicts in multiple countries. This is not because we love our wars, but regardless, we have to keep in mind that where there is a war, there are people who profit from it.

Being at war and being an aggressor are entirely different things. As long as we are not the aggressor, whether we should be at war depends on the particular cause. The war on drugs, even though it is not a real war per se, or part of the statistics above, was perhaps motivated by a just cause, but it has only added to the misery and socioeconomic issues that surround drugs. If there is one cause worth going to war for, it is cancer. And if we have to make it a profitable war for someone to win it, so be it.

Whether it is a family member, friend, neighbor, or associate, we all know someone who has suffered from cancer. I know at least four people within my immediate social circle who had cancer. We Americans have a one-in-three chance of developing cancer in our lifetime.

The American Cancer Society (cancer.org) estimates a total of 1,658,370 new cancer cases and 589,430 deaths due to cancer in the US in 2015. The death toll from cancer in 2015 alone is higher than the number of Americans who died in World War I, World War II, Vietnam, and Iraq combined. Please take a moment to think about this.*

Our government has been taking an increasingly active role concerning cancer research and cancer care. Survival rates are up by about 20%, to 68% in 2009, from 49% in 1978, but 68% is simply still not enough.* Perhaps, as was the case with drugs, we could have a cancer czar to orchestrate private and public activities. There may be more organizations working on cancer than on any other issue. So while there is no lack of grassroots efforts and institutional activities around cancer, the fact remains that 1,600 of us die each day due to cancer.*

I suggest that a National Cancer Registry (NCR) be created, perhaps by an existing organization such as the American

Cancer Society. While there are already a few dozen registries at the state and national levels, the purpose of this registry would be different. First, the NCR would consolidate information from all other registries under one roof. This aggregation of information would multiply the power of the database and do for cancer what Homeland Security has done for its areas of responsibility. Second, the registry would be open to the public (stripped of identifying information), allowing a better understanding and analysis of data and leading to the discovery of gaps in our approach that may not be so obvious today. Third, it would invite cancer patients to view and complete their information. The focus of this registry would be to find links between various types of cancers and lifestyle factors. These factors could include diets high in hormone-fed meats, the use of cellular phones, living in proximity to cellular antennas, or the use of smart digital meters, as well as less controversial factors such as smoking and sun tanning.

The estimated cost of cancer according to the NIH was over $216 billion, or about $700 per capita, in 2009.* Cancer should be at the forefront of our minds, and it would be great if one of the news networks could have daily updates on the topic. A five-minute segment could cover the latest successes, ongoing efforts, new organizations, experimental drugs, latest statistics, and other relevant information.

The proposed National Health and Biometric Database as well as the National Cancer Registry would streamline the collection of, access to, and use of available information on cancer. The proposed NHS would increase the probability of early detection. SAM would improve data gathering, communication, and analysis of new data. The engagement of

IBM's Watson by Memorial Sloan Kettering Cancer Center exemplifies such improvement even today. Watson presents evidence-based treatment options while sifting through millions of patient records in a matter of seconds.*

Our nation has a history of overcoming obstacles regardless of how hard they may seem and taking the lead to find solutions. We cannot simply let one third of our population suffer. As a nation, we need to come together and overcome this challenge.

40

Work to Live, Not Live to Work

★ ★ ★ ★

Throughout this book, we address various factors that affect our social and economic needs. To be happy, though, we need to change our attitude about work.

Regardless of our financial status, most of us live to work. If we do not make enough money, we work two or three jobs to make ends meet. If we are successful, we spend long days away from our families to keep our high-paying jobs.

We take our smartphones to bed with us and stay in touch with work at nights and on weekends. Yes, it is mostly expected of us—when you get a text from work late in the afternoon on Friday and wait until Monday to answer, you may get into trouble—but we are the ones who create such expectations. If we start taking our personal time more seriously, others will too.

I suggest the creation of a mandatory vacation/sick-leave system that requires employers to provide paid time off and requires employees to take it. Almost all employers provide some type of vacation or sick leave, but some employers never prepare themselves for the absence of their employees. As a result, employees may be hesitant to take time off and risk losing their status within the company. They may be worried about losing their jobs completely. Two-fifths of American workers leave their vacation time unused.*

Some employers pay for vacation time that is not taken, enabling employees to decide between taking time off or cashing in their vacation time. This may inadvertently encourage employees not to take time off in order to get paid more instead. Other employers let the accrued time expire to force employees to take time off. All of these rules have their own merits. The Family and Medical Leave Act (FMLA) requires companies with more than fifty employees to provide unpaid time off for certain events.* The FMLA does not cover all employees for all companies, but when it applies, the employee's job remains protected. This provides the necessary protection for companies with more than fifty employees and can serve as a guideline for all other companies.

Similar to the FMLA for unpaid time off, there should also be a minimum required amount of vacation and sick leave, such as two weeks or ten business days annually. This paid time off (PTO) should apply to all companies, even though this is typically an issue in smaller companies. Employers should be encouraged to increase this period as their employees invest more time in the company. Personally, as an employer, I have often combined vacation and sick leave days into one category of PTO, which is a great way to put employees in charge of managing time off and solve the problem of people calling in sick when all they really want is a day off.

It is not uncommon for small business owners to act as if they cannot afford for their employees to be away, and to think that productivity goes down when their employees are absent. These employers are most likely confusing the number of hours worked with productivity. On average, a secure, relaxed, and well-trained worker is much more productive than one who is stressed and overworked. Taking care of employees and arranging for their time off is an investment in a business's greatest asset: productive and conscientious employees. Furthermore, small businesses should be encouraged, while not required, to follow the FMLA guidelines to the best of their abilities and provide PTO to both genders for childbirth, bereavement of an immediate family member, and other major life events.

Employees should take full advantage of their time away from work to achieve a more balanced life. At the same time, while at work they should use their time productively and fulfill their roles responsibly. Companies of all sizes are constantly under pressure to perform, and small businesses heavily rely on their employees to succeed. Large corporations face challenges to compete globally in order to maintain and grow their market share. Each person who works for a company helps make that company what it is, so everyone at a company has to work conscientiously in order to prosper collectively.

Here is a piece of advice that I have offered to my employees:

We become what we put into our work, so put in 120% and become that much more productive. If one day your employer is not appreciative of what you put in, you will have much more to offer to your next potential employer.

41

National Holidays

★ ★ ★ ★

A few months after I arrived in the US, I was invited for lunch at my cousin's house. It was a holiday and I wanted to buy him something, but the streets of Dallas were deserted. I drove to the mall, where I found the parking lot totally empty. On the way to his house, the only store I found open was 7-Eleven. When I arrived at his house, I told him that no one was on the road and that everything was closed. He said, "Of course, it's Thanksgiving!"

Now, some thirty years later, there is not one holiday when everything is closed. In fact, some stores stay open all night to get a head start on their Black Friday sales. Black Friday should be a day when we mourn the loss of our values! We should all be ashamed for embracing this practice, both the shoppers who enable it and the CEOs and members of the board of directors at big corporations that have perpetrated it.

I suggest that we not shop on our major holidays, such as Thanksgiving, Christmas, and New Year's Day. They are meant for us to give thanks for our blessings, celebrate what we believe in, and renew our commitments to ourselves and each other.

If we paid any attention to what's happening to us as a people, we would start taking these holidays as a chance to spend time with our loved ones and reflect upon our lives. By making this simple change, we can enjoy our holidays and allow others to enjoy theirs too. We should not allow ourselves to shop on certain holidays, no matter how tempting it may be. If enough of us did this, with the first holiday sales report some changes would be made, and by the second or the third year companies would conclude that it is not cost effective to keep stores open on major holidays. The mega-sales will still be there the next day.

42

Social Security and Retirement

★ ★ ★ ★

We must not measure the success of our society and its citizens by the cars we drive, the houses we own, or the positions we hold, but by our happiness. Although what makes us happy is a philosophical discussion beyond the scope of this book, it is also a social and financial discussion. The perspectives on this question may vary greatly from one person to another. If we define success by how well we, the majority of the population, as well as those we push to the margins of society, live, then we can measure it as a function of satisfying our needs. In the free and democratic society where we live, our needs vary considerably, but we all have certain basic necessities. Since these necessities can be defined for our entire society, our government can help ensure their availability. However, our needs are different at each stage of life. When we are young, we need strong laws to protect us against predators. We need parents or guardians who can take care of us. We need a formal education since we can no longer survive on instinct alone. As we grow up, we need the means to support ourselves and pay for food and shelter. Finally, as we get older, we need more care. Throughout all stages of life, we also need medical care to stay healthy. Thus far, we have discussed ways to address all of our needs except for retirement, which we will address here.

Social Security is the best way to create the minimum level of support during retirement, but it's just the minimum. We have to maintain this minimum, but Social Security may be facing financial issues. The extent and urgency of these issues are not simply determined by the current annual deficit as some would like us to believe, but by the size of the fund, the inflow of revenues, and the outflow of benefits over many years.*

The inflow, or the revenue generated through taxation, depends on our productivity or factors such as the state of the economy, the size of US workforce, and the retirement age. The factors affecting the outflow, or total benefits paid, include the number of recipients, benefits paid, the retirement age, and life expectancy. A surplus or deficit is the difference between the inflow and outflow of capital, but this alone does not define the state of Social Security.

We had a $77 billion deficit in 2014, which indicates that for the provided benefits that year, our productivity was too low, or that for the level of productivity, the total paid in benefits was too high.* However, we cannot assume that either our productivity or benefits will remain the same or that several years of deficit mean that the Social Security program is no longer feasible.

To have a better understanding of the fund, we can compare it to the radiator reservoir in your car. When your car heats up (productivity is high), the reservoir may get filled (surplus), and when it is cooled down, the reservoir may partially empty (deficit), but the fluctuation in the reservoir is the reason the reservoir (fund) exists in the first place and is part of its normal function. It is not an indicator of how well the Social Security program functions. Only when deficit becomes a trend and the reservoir becomes empty might we have a problem. Even then, as long as the engine (economy) runs well, we will be fine. Nevertheless, we will explore ways to keep the reservoir filled.

President Roosevelt created Social Security in 1935. Social Security consists of three programs: retirement, survivor, and disability.* Under the retirement program, one receives a monthly income from Social Security once he or she reaches age 67, if born in 1960 or later, or he or she may opt to receive partial income starting at age 62.* The amount received depends on one's contribution or income from working. The survivor program pays for the surviving spouse at retirement age as well as their children under the age of eighteen; while disability pays those who are disabled.

We pay 6.2% of our income, up to $118,500, in Social Security taxes, which is matched by our employers. This number is known as the wage base, which has gradually been increased from $3,000 in 1937.* So, if we make $50,000, we pay $3,100 in Social Security taxes, and our employer pays $3,100; therefore the Social Security Trust Fund receives

$6,200. If we make $118,500, we pay $7,347, our employer makes a matching contribution, and the Social Security Trust Fund receives $14,694. The contribution is capped at this amount, even if we earn $200,000 or a million. This is the inflow side of Social Security, how social security gets funded.

On the outflow, or benefit side, one has to reach retirement age to receive Social Security benefits in full unless one is disabled or a surviving spouse. Since income received from Social Security is based on one's earnings, to qualify, one must work forty quarters (ten years) and earn at least $1,200.00 in each quarter. Calculating how much one receives is not simple, but to provide you with a sense of it, here are two examples: In both cases, the recipient was born in 1945, is seventy in 2015, has worked for thirty years, from 1985 to the end of 2014, and has made the same amount each year. If he made $100,000, he would receive $3,245 a month or $38,940 a year. If his annual income was $20,000 a year, he would receive $1,575 a month or $18,900 a year. These figures are gross incomes, and you can assume a reduction of 23 cents on a dollar due to taxes. You can use the Social Security Administration website to estimate your income.*

As a side note, someone who has consistently made $100,000 will be forced to live with $38,940 per year, or 38% of the income he or she is accustomed to, while someone making $20,000 will receive $18,900 (95%), or almost exactly the same income. I am simply pointing out that Social Security is indeed social security and not a retirement plan, since most people cannot solely rely on it for their retirement.

When the program was created, the average life expectancy was sixty-one and the retirement age was sixty-five.* In

1930, the number of Americans sixty-five years or older was 6.7 million; while in 2000, this number was 34.9 million.* While some point to these statistics as shocking news, there is nothing newsworthy about them. It is a trend that has been anticipated, and the fund is there exactly for this reason. In other words, we have paid more in taxes to build the fund, knowing that this day would come.

So neither the deficit in the fund nor the number of people living way past retirement age should be cause for alarm. But what if the trend continues? A man or woman reaching sixty-five years of age now is expected to live to 84.3 and 86.6 respectively. One out of four Americans lives past the age of ninety and one out of ten lives past ninety-five. What if GRIN technologies (genetics, robotics, information, and nanotechnology) allow us to live to be 150?* Do we still retire at sixty-seven? Reaching a much higher life expectancy is within the range of possibilities.

I do not believe that benefits should be cut directly, by paying out less, or indirectly, by tweaking the CPI (consumer price index) or freezing the purchasing power of Social Security.* As we mentioned earlier, a dollar in 1971 was worth less than nineteen cents in 2012, so the benefits have already been cut even after considering the CPI.*

However, I do believe that the retirement age should be linked to the average life expectancy, while early retirement should remain at sixty-two. To do this, I would leave the current retirement age for anyone born before 1960. This means that anyone who is currently 55 years or older can retire when 67. For those born after 1960, I would peg their retirement age to the life expectancy by adding a month to their retirement age for every two months increase in life expectancy over 80. So let's assume that in year 2020 the average life expectancy will become ninety. This will make the retirement age seventy-two (67+ [(90-80)/2]). The adjustments may be made gradually on an annual basis.

When we do this, we have to consider that if someone starts working at twenty-two, he or she will have already worked for fifty years before retiring at seventy-two. The question may become then, why not increase the age of early retirement? My reasoning is that the average life expectancy is just an average and not everyone lives to be that age; yet everyone pays Social Security taxes. People who do not expect to live as long due to their health or other reasons should still have some retirement. If the early retirement age is increased by five years, we will reduce the number of people who can take advantage of it by about 2.5%.*

When we increase the retirement age, we do not just reduce spending, we also increase revenues since it is more likely a person will remain active. Additional revenues can be created by removing the wage base. I suggest removing the Social Security wage base, or the ceiling on wages subject to Social Security deductions. Social Security taxes are collected as a percentage of any gross income below the wage base, which is $118,500 in 2015.

Removing the wage cutoff for Social Security deductions would have no effect on anyone who earns less than $118,500 a year now, which is the case for the majority of the population. It would, however, have adverse effects on small businesses since employers match their employees' contributions.

To remedy this problem, we need to create an exemption for small businesses.

In order to exempt small businesses, we need to define a small business. Since Social Security taxes are based on employees' salaries and not a company's revenues or profits, we can define a small business by its number of full-time and part-time employees and contractors.

Although companies do not pay taxes or Social Security on contractors' wages, we should still include contractors for this purpose. This would ensure that there is no incentive to classify a worker as a contractor to avoid paying Social Security. We can use a number such as one hundred employees (full-time, part-time, or contractors) as the threshold.

Now that we have defined a small business, I propose that small businesses' Social Security contributions be limited to the wage base. In other words, I propose that the wage base be removed for all employees regardless of company size. For small businesses, however, the employers' wage base cutoff point would still exist. With this change, whoever earns an annual income of $118,500 or less will see no change. However, those who make more will pay Social Security taxes proportionate to their salaries. For example, someone who earns $200,000 would pay $12,200 rather than $7,347. His or her employer would pay $7,347 if it is a small business or $12,200 otherwise. In this example, the total Social Security taxes collected will be $19,547 if it is a small business and $24,400 otherwise.

Removing the Social Security wage base may seem unfair for those who make more than $118,500 a year. After all, if the benefits that we receive from Social Security are capped, shouldn't our contribution be capped as well?

Most of us fundamentally accept the idea that society should expect more from someone who is more knowledgeable. For example, we hold lawyers to higher standards when it comes to respecting the law because of their knowledge of the law. The same is true for other professionals, such as physicians and accountants. At the other extreme, one's lack of knowledge or low IQ can be used as a defense in a court of law. However, we do not apply the same logic to wealth. If we earn a higher salary than most of the population, it is because we have spent more time at school, or because we are smarter or work harder, or simply because we deserve it. While we may deserve to make more money, we can do so only because society has enabled us. Even if we went to a private university and paid for all our own expenses, the university has benefited from society and its top faculty are products of what our taxes have enabled. Many tech millionaires and billionaires have become successful because they were smart, but also because our infrastructure enabled them to achieve their goals. The very Internet that has enabled most technologies is a product of public funding. So contributing to Social Security without a wage base as the cutoff point simply returns the favor.

Having kept the retirement age for the current and soon-to-be retirees, the benefits, and the solvency of the Social Security Trust Fund, we now will address how the trust fund should be maintained; that is, how to hold the money or how to invest it. While we can debate whether or not our government should manage the Social Security Trust Fund, we absolutely cannot privatize it or hand it over to Wall Street.

Currently the Social Security Trust Fund is invested in special-issue government bonds, which are backed by our trust in the government. While that may seem inadequate, this trust has the same backing that our money enjoys. So on one hand, the Social Security Trust Fund is as secure as our money, but on the other hand, this means that the fate of our Social Security is in the hands of the government and — just as is the case with our money — in the hands of bankers.

I suggest that the Social Security Trust Fund be invested in mortgages secured by high-equity real estate. The lower the loan-to-property value, the higher the equity and lower the risk. A typical mortgage is worth 75–80% of the value of the property used to secure it at the time the loan is obtained — leaving only 20–25% in equity. As payments are made, the loan-to-property value ratio decreases and the mortgage becomes more secure.

The Social Security Trust Fund should acquire mortgages with a 50% ratio, meaning that the value of the property is twice as much as that of the mortgage. While this almost guarantees a payoff and drastically reduces risks, it would not be practical for buyers since they would have to pay half of the property's value up front in cash in order to secure a mortgage. However, this type of mortgage is a practical option for refinancing an existing mortgage that has reached the 50% threshold. Mortgages may be issued for repayment in ten, fifteen, twenty, or thirty years with low interest rates. In practice, the Social Security Trust Fund will buy such mortgages in bulk directly from banks.

There are multiple benefits of the Social Security Trust Fund investing in high-equity mortgages. First, the trust fund will no longer be backed by our trust in the government, but rather by a tangible asset. Second, the low-interest mortgages create a fixed income return for the trust fund, allowing the fund to at least keep up with inflation. Third, the housing market will become less exposed to the manipulations of Wall Street and the banking system. Fourth, the low-interest mortgages will increase household savings. Lastly, home ownership will become more affordable, thereby strengthening the fabric of our communities, lowering crime rates, and increasing middle-class economic power.

With these changes we should be able to maintain our Social Security Trust Fund's solvency, but Social Security still provides only a minimum level of income needed in retirement. To maintain one's standard of living, there are various tax-deferred retirement investment accounts such as 401(k) plans or employee stock ownership plans (ESOP). Some of these plans, such as the 401(k), allow employees to contribute a portion of their income to their retirement account, which then grows tax-free.* At retirement one can withdraw the savings and then pay taxes on them. If the funds are prematurely withdrawn, they will be subject to taxes and penalties. Most often, companies that offer their employees these retirement accounts also match a portion of their employees' contribution. There are other various retirement accounts accommodating self-employment, transferring accounts, etc., and they may have different tax rules.

Although retirement accounts, especially those with matching contributions from employers, can provide considerable financial support, they are far from an ideal solution. The 401(k) investment accounts are not offered by all employers, often because they are costly to set up and maintain. When they are offered, the amount that can be contributed is a percentage of one's compensation, subject to certain caps. The investment options vary from one provider to another, and they are limited and sometimes costly. Most of these accounts allow employees the flexibility to borrow against their accounts, paying interest on the amount borrowed. About one out of five employees exercises this option when the borrowing is allowed. The most popular retirement plans, 401(k)s are worth at least $4.4 trillion, or 18% of the $24 trillion in US retirement assets as of June 30, 2014.* In 2012, there were 515,000 401(k) plans with about 52 million participants.

ESOPs allow companies, at their discretion, to contribute, on an annual basis, cash or their stocks into a trust held by employees. In this fashion, ESOPs allow employees to work for their own company—even though the ownership varies greatly. For tax reasons, ESOPs work better for private companies than publicly traded ones. Statistically, employees who invest in their ESOPs have higher balances than those who invest in 401(k) plans on average. However, ESOPs are riskier since the entire value of the employee's portfolio is invested in a single company. Even more so when considering that this single company is also paying their salary. Should something happen to this company, employees may find themselves without a paycheck and without their retirement funds. The best scenario is when companies offer both 401(k) and ESOP retirement accounts.

I suggest that 401(k)s and ESOPs be kept mostly as they are, but that the investment options in 401(k)s be standardized. This standardization will cause investment options to be analyzed, compared, and evaluated more thoroughly, thus leading to better options and investments.

While retirement accounts such as 401(k)s or ESOPs are great, the problem is that only 53% of American workers have a retirement account. Another problem with these accounts is that the contribution is a percentage of the compensation. That is why I also recommend profit-sharing retirement accounts. The profit-sharing accounts contribute to the employee's retirement account based on the company's net profit rather than on the employee's compensation. They can be offered in addition to or in place of an ESOP or 401(k) plan. Personally, as an employer, I would prefer to share the profit of a company with my employees rather than offering a 401(k) account. The latter is a fixed cost to a company regardless of the company's performance. On the other hand, the profit sharing apportions profits that employees helped generate.

The profit-sharing amount could be set up as a percentage of the company's annual profit nationally. This percentage would be the same for all companies. In each quarter, companies would contribute this percentage to employees' profit-sharing accounts. Employees could be ranked by the number of years they have worked for the company as well as by their positions. The ranking would range from one to ten, with one being an entry-level position and ten for executives or employees who have been with the company for ten years or more. The available pool of money would be divided by the number of employees and their ranking, so if there are a hundred employees with an average ranking of five, the pool would be divided by five hundred. Then each employee receives a multiple of this amount based on his or her ranking; for example, an employee with a rank of seven receives seven times as much as one with a ranking of one. The net amount after taxes is deposited into the employee's retirement account.

There are multiple benefits to implementing profit-sharing retirement plans. To start, the amount paid is part of the company's profits and is not a fixed cost. This could make all the difference for a company going through tough times. Second, since this is a profit-sharing plan, the company can afford to hold onto its employees longer in hard economic conditions, since if there is no profit, there is also no requirement to pay profit-sharing benefits. Employees may feel that this is a disadvantage to them, but they should consider that if the company does not survive, there will be no jobs, no ESOPs, and in some cases, a decrease in the value of their 401(k). Third, profit sharing becomes a motivating factor for employees to be efficient, generate profits, and to stay with a company in order to maintain and improve their ranking. Fourth, during downsizing, companies would have no incentive to get rid of high-ranking employees in order to save, since the same amount of money would go to other employees rather than reverting to the company. Fifth, employees who are not high on the pay scale would have a chance to earn as much in profit sharing as an executive by improving their rank. Additionally, since the contribution to profit-sharing accounts would be made after deducting taxes, it would not affect tax revenue.

43

Second Home

★ ★ ★ ★

According to recent statistics, there are more than 1.6 million homeless children in America today.* If our society is to overcome some of its most crucial issues and be able to feel proud of itself, we must not leave anyone behind. At the top of that list are our children and our elderly. Providing a shelter for homeless and neglected children is an investment in our country's future.

As our life expectancy increases, so does the need to take care of our aging citizens. We all hope that we will be taken care of when we can no longer care for ourselves, and we usually look to our children for health, emotional, or financial care. However, not everyone is capable of taking care of his or her aging parents, so we need to offer some options in those cases.

I suggest that we build a national network of accommodations, starting with one location in every state, and gradually grow them to multiple locations. This national network of second homes would not be a governmental entity, but a nonprofit organization funded through our contributions. These centers would house both children and senior citizens under one roof. Children would benefit from these centers until they become nineteen years old, which is when they should graduate from college. We discussed this in earlier chapters.

Allowing children and the elderly to live under one roof creates a symbiotic relationship between the two. The elderly would provide help and wisdom to the young, depending on their physical and mental condition, as well as their background and practical skills; teenagers would return the favor by assisting the elderly and the young. The center would benefit from interactions among various age groups. The young would have access to the elders' invaluable lifetime experience, while the elderly would benefit from their interactions with younger and more active residents. That interaction is certain to improve the older residents' mental and physical conditions.

As you read this, you may be thinking that you would not want your parents to be around troubled youth as some of the current homeless children may be. If that's the case, it means that you have other options available to you and this may not be for you. Troubled children are not born that way. Homelessness, no sense of belonging, no guidance, and toxic surroundings are often the source of their problems. Some of the programs that I am suggesting, such as Second Home, may take a long time to produce the desired result—perhaps as long as a generation—but a child growing up in the Second Home should not be a troubled child.

44

Morality, Legality, Normality

★ ★ ★ ★

This book is mainly about making changes in the law to improve our legal, financial, and social structure so that we can live better, but if we believe that the law alone is sufficient to improve our lives, we are sorely mistaken. Although morality is the basis of some of our laws, our society cannot succeed based on laws alone. It also must rely on morality, mercy, and compassion. Morality and integrity are intertwined, but for the purpose of this book, I would like to define integrity as being honest, truthful, and sincere, and morality as the difference between right and wrong. As such, a prostitute may have integrity, while parting with morality.

We desperately try to keep church and state separate, but we expect our elected officials to be moral role models. We have to correct these expectations. Our elected officials must excel at what they are elected to do and keep their promises to the people. Our officials must be role models for integrity, but not morality. They must be competent and carry out their duties and keep their pledges, but they should not be our role models from any other perspectives. For example, a sexual affair involving one of our elected officials should be kept between the elected official and his or her family. When the same affair involves one's subordinate, then it will become an integrity issue and our business as well.

Our children's role models for morality should be their parents, grandparents, and faith leaders, and while some of us may like to take the easy way out and pass that responsibility to our officials or celebrities, this does not work. Being a role model for our children does not necessarily imply that we must be flawless. Nobody is flawless. It simply means that they need to know what is right and what is wrong about us.

To create values in our society, we have to start with families; parents need to instill morals in their children. The law may deter our children from doing wrong, but it is nothing in comparison to their much more powerful and omnipresent moral inner voice. For example, if children believe that cheating is wrong, they will not cheat. But if they believe that it is okay to cheat, they will do so if they are certain they will not get caught.

Besides morality, integrity, and legality, there is another factor that plays a critical role in our lives: normality—what society believes is normal or what it accepts as a normal behavior. It takes years to change what we consider normal, and this also begins with the family. Bribery is a good example to explore here. Bribery is unethical since it unfairly tips the scales in favor of the briber. Bribery is also illegal in most countries.

Therefore, it is both illegal and unethical; yet it is how people do business in numerous countries around the world. Luckily, so far, bribery has been an exception in the US, not the norm.

To improve our society, we need to raise the bar regarding what is considered normal and lower it on what is legal. For example, our society expects us to be on time when arriving at an event. That is a social norm, and we generally follow the norm to be socially accepted. Now, if we introduced a system that imposed a fee on someone who was late, we would be discounting the social element. By simply imposing a fine, the need to be on time would no longer exist. People would no longer need to be on time; they would only need to balance the time they would like to arrive and the fine they would like to pay. This result was, in fact, observed in an experiment in which parents were fined when they picked up their children late from daycare.* This example is intended to demonstrate that sometimes the shame incurred by breaking the norm can be the most powerful incentive to do what is right, and that we can promote positive behavior by expecting it; hence raising the bar on what is the norm.

So, that may justify raising the bar on the norm, but why should we lower the bar on what is legal? The simple answer is that the resources spent enforcing laws rather than establishing norms can be spent on more important issues that cannot be managed by morals. Moral norms do not prevent our children from getting shot at school. However, the right values prevent our children from cheating, smoking, gambling, or becoming violent.

Simply stated, while I stand for legalizing matters that I consider immoral, I do so to address larger issues and to remove what I consider to be means of control and manipulation. Therefore, it is critical that we raise the bar on what is considered normal and acceptable.

While our forefathers clearly attempted to keep church and state separate, it would have been difficult for them to envision a godless society. After the Gulf War, the friction among religions has been increasing. I believe that the purpose of all religions is to instill good in people and enhance our lives, and as such, I believe that extremists destroy faith regardless of what teachings they follow. As individuals and as a society, we should believe in a higher power, understand our equality under God, and use our faith to better ourselves and our surroundings. Only then can we improve our lives. Believing in a higher power and accepting our equality have broad effects on the way we treat ourselves, each other, and even our environment.

There are different views as to how the human race came to be. As we become more advanced, we demystify and gain even more understanding about how our universe works, but in the end, nothing explains who started it all. If we inspect a demolished fifty-story high-rise, we can deduce what came first and what came next and what caused what, but we cannot tell who pulled the trigger. I call the one who pulled the trigger to our existence God, and when I look at his creation, I deduce that he is almighty and all-powerful. He is omnipresent and his domain goes beyond space and time.

Now suppose that there is a genius roboticist who builds a self-contained factory in which robots build other robots. They are built to repair, maintain, disassemble, and recycle each other, to guide and orchestrate their activities, to plan and design new and better robots, and so on. So this robotic ecosystem is self-sufficient, and the robots are constantly being assembled for their roles and disassembled into raw parts that may be used to build new robots. It would be fascinating to watch this factory!

Let's further suppose that our genius roboticist figures out that rather than building this factory, he can just start it with a mass. Not just any mass, but one so ingenious that when it explodes, it starts expanding and creating new elements from old elements, combining elements into each other in every possible way, and putting each combination into its own use.

Years later, when we look at the factory and see how everything is, we are not only fascinated by how things are but impressed at how simple yet sophisticated their evolution has been. It is impressive that everything works together, but it is even more mind-boggling to understand how everything has come to be. We witness the death of one robot as it results in the formation of another, even better robot, and we remain in awe. We know this is an intelligent design, and every further discovery and understanding, whether of natural selection or the big bang theory, only adds awesome factors to the design.

If, in an opening break shot of billiards, the balls, instead of randomly sitting in the pockets or on the pool table, gathered to form a snowflake, we would not accept the idea that the balls had randomly formed a snowflake. Instead, we would believe that some kind of power had been involved in getting the balls into that shape. So it should not be unreasonable to believe that there is a power behind the formation of the universe.

The universe is simply a much larger pool table. It is so vast that if we traveled at many times the speed of light, even though such speed is not possible according to Einstein's theory, we would never leave our galaxy, the Milky Way, since it is 100,000 light years across. Simply put, it would take us 100,000 years to cross our own galaxy at the speed of light. The universe is so vast, in fact, that if our solar system, one of at least 100,000,000,000 out there, were a football field, earth and all its inhabitants would be the size of a grain of table salt.

I am not evangelizing faith, but making a point that believing in a higher power is not only reasonable but also beneficial. From a philosophical stance, it makes no difference to the higher power whether we believe in it or not, but believing makes a difference for us. It connects us to an infinite source of power. Imagine that you knew President Obama and you could pick up the phone and call him anytime. Regardless of the president's response, try to imagine how you would feel knowing that you have such an access. Now that's just access to another mortal being without any power over the universe. Believing in the ultimate power is the most powerful foundation one can build upon. It is empowering. We are simply better off believing than not!

So believing is another factor and component in our happiness. We have talked about how to fix our government, our money, our education, our retirement, our healthcare system, and more. We also talked about our attitudes and what's considered normal. It takes many factors to live a balanced, happy life. Believing is another factor, and it's free and available to everyone.

45

Government and Taxes

★ ★ ★ ★

When we think of government, we may automatically think of bureaucracy, waste, and inefficiencies. A Republican may describe the US government as too big while a Democrat may think of it as not big enough or not doing enough. If you have read up to this chapter, you may think that my proposals require money that we do not have, that they are not affordable, and that government that may be too big regardless of your political alignment. Let's address the latter first.

First and foremost, I believe that the government should represent every citizen, from the billionaires to the homeless, from the philosophers to the illiterate, from the saints to the sinners, and from the lawmakers to those on death row, and it should do so equally and selflessly. By that alone, justice will be served, equality will be restored, citizens will be nurtured, and prosperity will ensue.

In serving everyone, our government must be strong

enough to take on any entity, foreign or domestic, that stands on its way. While we have military supremacy, the danger to our way of life will not likely be foreign, but domestic. To represent us equally, our government must be able to take on bankers, billionaires, conglomerate corporations, and special interest groups. To do this selflessly, it must cleanse itself of political greed and self-serving parties and hold itself accountable, avail itself of strong ethics, and use them to serve its people.

We desperately need this government representation now, and our needs grow as the disparity of wealth grows. In almost every chapter of this book, you can find scenarios from which only our government can protect us. The US budget for the year 2015 is $3.9 trillion, which is 21.8% of its $17.9 trillion GDP.* As we discussed earlier, the market cap of the twelve largest banks in the US is $1.32 trillion, and their assets are $11.8 trillion.* As large as banks are, there are only three banks on the list of top twenty companies by market caps. The list includes companies such as Apple, Exxon, Microsoft, Google, Walmart, GE, Chevron, Verizon, Facebook, and Coca-Cola among others.* Every mega-corporation, every billionaire, and every interest group wants a smaller government so they can have their way. If you wish for small government, be careful what you wish for!

If we compare our government to a business, its size should not be questioned. We do not say Walmart is too big or too small. We ask what its business is or, in the case of the government, what its responsibilities are. As such, the government needs only to be large enough to carry its responsibilities. Of course, a big government does not translate to a responsible one, and a small government does mean a weak one. The concept of this book started with the financial crash of 2008 and the lack of action by our government. One theory is that our justice department had the will but not the might to go after the banks.* We have to ensure that this does not happen again.

So how do we ensure that a big government is a responsible government? One criticism that I've received from a book critic is that I am too trusting of our elected officials and too naïve about what we can get done. That trust may stem from two facts: there are more good people than bad ones by far, and we are still a democracy.

Bad people, like bad news, get more publicity precisely because they are not common. If I ask you to name as many major events from 2014 as you can, you may recall a few disasters, such as those involving Malaysia Airlines flights. These ill-fated flights took the spotlight, though over thirty million commercial flights safely completed their journeys in 2014.* That taking of the spotlight also applies to bad people.

Regarding democracy, we are the government. We don't have a king or his appointees presiding over us. We are the ones electing our representatives, and we can ensure our freedom in three different ways: cast our votes at the ballot box, voice our votes, and act our votes. We need to use social media and the other numerous channels available to us to protect our rights. Then we need to act as we believe. If we enjoy seeing Christmas tree lots and pumpkin patches, we should shop there even if we pay a few dollars more. If we want stores to close on holidays, we must stop shopping on holidays. If we want better food, we should start by buying food with safer ingredients. Yes, I believe that we can correct our course, and that brings us to the next topic: Where does the money for my proposals come from?

Out of all my proposals, a few require funding, or more funding than is available now.

Education reform, which includes the reduction of K–12 to K–10, the addition of Spanish, the creation of a national curriculum, and providing a three-year vocational degree, does not require funding. It requires reshuffling resources and creating efficiencies through a standardization of the K–10 curriculum as well the implementation of courses through Educational Virtual Attendants (EVA).

The money saved from not fighting illicit drugs or prostitution would be used to fight cancer, child pornography, and white-collar crimes.

We recommended ways to have a better retirement system without adding the cost to the public.

We included the budget for the Independent Reporting Organization into the defense budget and made it one tenth of one percent of the defense budget.

The National Health and Biometric Database (NHBD) as well as the National Healthcare System (NHS) require funding. The cost of Healthcare.gov, the official website for Obamacare, may be above $600 million.* Let's remember that this website, similar to health insurance companies, is not healthcare! It does not advance medicine, and it does not reduce the cost of healthcare. In fact, in addition to its startup cost of $667 million, there will be ongoing administrative costs.

This is perhaps the major difference between a business and a government. James Clark, a businessman, founded

WebMD with $16 million of his money and some additional funding from investors.* To do so, he researched and understood what was missing and needed in the market, and came up with the best way of providing it. He launched a business that now has a market cap of over $1.5 billion (as of January 2015), $305 million in profit, and 32.3 million unique users per month.** A website that started with tens of millions has profited many times over, and over 30 million users a month turn to it for issues concerning their health. I wonder what James Clark or IBM's Watson could do with over $600 million.

So, even when our government agrees with us about policies, there is disagreement about their implementation. Let's assume that everyone should have access to healthcare. The government's response has been to build yet another heavy layer of administration on top of the for-profit insurance companies to provide us this access. Be it Obamacare, Republican care, no care, or the NHS, we the taxpayers always pay for it.

As we always pay for it, then the question should be how to make it more efficient. The subject of efficiency should be at the forefront of the healthcare system. The NHBD, the NHS, and SAM are all about efficiencies and reducing costs. The total cost of these services would be less than what we now pay with Obamacare or what we paid prior to Obamacare, and would be paid for through taxation. That bring us to taxes and where I stand philosophically.

To start, I do not believe in a trickle-down economy. This is my analogy of a trickle-down economy: We want to water our crops so we let the water in our pond evaporate to form clouds, and we hope that it rains on the crops. That's not how we irrigate our crops, and that's not how our economy should work. This simply means that I support our progressive tax system, in which the more you make, the higher your tax bracket is. Unfortunately, higher brackets do not always translate to higher taxes.

On the other hand, I do not believe that our government should be in the business of charity. The government, regardless of its efforts, will never be good or efficient at charitable work. We all need a certain level of education, whether we are poor or rich or black or white. All of us also need healthcare, and we often are the victim of our genetics, social status, incidents, or accidents. Therefore, these services should be available to everyone and paid for through taxation. However, when it comes to other needs, such as food and shelter, the government should support policies that ensure equal treatment and opportunity, but otherwise, it should leave the charity work for nonprofit organizations. We should have higher minimum wages and time off from work, and we should continue enforcing anti-discrimination laws to ensure work for anyone who is willing to work. We need to provide affordable loans to encourage home-ownership. Nonprofit organizations and grassroots efforts should take care of food and shelter for the needy, and our tax code should allow contributions to these organizations even more than it does now.

Some of the proposals in this book are designed to stop waste and fraud. These proposals include the Financial Transparency Service, Freedom Watch, the Independent Reporting Organization, and the NHS.

Finally, we suggested changing the US monetary system, which is a hole in our pockets today.

Now, let's talk about our tax codes. Nearly everyone agrees, perhaps for different reasons, that the American tax code should be simplified. My primary reason for simplifying the code is to close loopholes. Imagine if the entire tax system could be defined in fewer than ten pages! It would become easy to see if the playing field is level. In general, our progressive tax system could be maintained if simplified. Suggesting actual tax rates is beyond the scope of this book. However, following are the principles of a proposed tax system that takes into account other changes recommended throughout this book.

- The tax code for both individuals and corporations should be simple enough to fit into five to ten pages of text.
- Every individual and every profitable corporation should pay taxes.
- Any money earned should be taxable regardless of how it is earned, so the same tax rate applies whether the source of income is salary, interest, dividends, capital gains, etc.
- All tax loopholes, tax credits, and alternative minimum tax should be eliminated.
- The same rate should apply to an individual regardless of his or her marital status; whether an individual is married, single, or the head of the household should not make a difference. Married couples should have the option of filing separately or jointly, but when filing jointly, their incomes should be combined and divided by two to determine their bracket.

- Gross income should be adjusted considering the following:
  - ◆ Medical expenses, including health insurance premiums as long as there is no NHS available, may be deducted. When the NHS is implemented, the health insurance premium would not be deductible.
  - ◆ Up to $25,000 may be contributed to tax-deferred retirement accounts regardless of the compensation or the type of retirement account.
  - ◆ Up to 10% of income may be contributed to a public charity that uses the Financial Transparency Service. This limit is to encourage contributions to the funds that serve everyone, including Social Security and the NHS.
  - ◆ Any amount of income may be contributed to Social Security and the NHS, which replaces Medicaid and Medicare.
  - ◆ All other deductions should be eliminated, including mortgage interest, assuming that low-interest mortgages become available through the government and the Social Security Trust Fund. Otherwise, mortgage interest on mortgage loans for a primary residence up to $500,000 may be deducted.
- The adjusted income cannot be less than 50% of the gross income.
- Estate tax: The exemption amount for 2015 is $5.43 million, which should remain as is and be adjusted annually according to the rate of inflation. The estate tax after the exempted amount should be reduced from

40% to 20%. The higher estate tax does not translate to the collection of higher taxes; instead it encourages finding ways to avoid paying taxes altogether.*

- No change in gift tax. The current tax-free gift amount is $14,000. This amount should be adjusted annually for inflation. Additionally, charitable, educational, medical, and political gifts, and gifts to spouses are exempt.*
- A 6.2% deduction for Social Security without the wage base except for small-business employers.
- NHS tax: Currently, we pay 1.45% of our income for Medicaid and Medicare, which is matched by the employer. Medicaid and Medicare will be replaced by the NHS and will be available to all citizens from cradle to grave. Under Obamacare, employers are asked to provide health insurance or face fines, with certain exceptions. An employer pays $4,266 annually on average to cover an employee, while an employee pays $1,118.* The annual out-of-pocket expense per household is $3,301, or about $1,650 per employee assuming two workers per household.* That brings the employee's portion to about $2,768 annually. Assuming an annual median individual income of $28,155, the cost of insurance as a percentage of an employee's income is 15% for the employer and 10% for the employee.* Each also pays 1.45% for Medicaid and Medicare; so on average, our employers pay 16.5% and we pay 11.5% of our income for health insurance. These numbers are estimates without consideration for Obamacare's subsidies. As we discussed, Obamacare

adds an administrative expense to the overall cost of the healthcare. We pay for this additional cost, so these numbers will be even higher. I would guesstimate that the NHS would reduce the total cost of healthcare by 30–50%. These are estimates since the actual calculations are beyond the scope of my resources and this book. With these figures in mind, I would suggest that we have a 5–7% NHS payroll tax that applies to all employees regardless of their income, instead of the 1.45% Medicare and Medicaid tax. Then the remaining cost of healthcare will be paid for by profitable corporations. We will do this by dividing the remaining cost of healthcare by the total annual profit of all US corporations and arrive at a percentage. Then we collect this percentage as NHS taxes on the profit of each company. This NHS corporate tax replaces companies' current cost of insuring their employees. For example, if the deficit (the remaining cost of the NHS after collecting all US employees' NHS payroll taxes) is $10 and the total profit of corporations in 2014 is $1,000, we divide 10 by 1000 and arrive at one percent. Then, we collect a one-percent tax from each company as NHS corporate tax. Further shortages may be collected as copay, as discussed in the NHS chapter.

For corporate taxes, I would suggest the following:

- Keep all existing corporate tax brackets of 15–35%.
- Add NHS tax as described above. This would be a special-purpose tax to fund any deficit in the NHS budget,

which would vary each year. The percentage may be determined based on the prior year's profit.

- Eliminate any and all tax credits except credits for income tax paid to foreign governments. Corporations may deduct income tax paid to foreign governments up to the amount they would have owed under the US tax system.
- Eliminate tax deferral.
- If a corporation's calculated tax rate falls below the minimum tax bracket of 15%, the 15% rate would apply. No corporation should pay less than 15% in income tax.

46

Pit Stop 3

★ ★ ★ ★

We turned our attention to the concentration of wealth and proposed a law to protect our freedom by capping capitalism. By removing the threat of extreme capitalism, providing accurate and current information, and making changes to the election process to restore a government "by the people, for the people," we can prevent further deterioration of our freedom. Now we can turn our attention to making changes that will address our social and economic issues, in the hope that our children will have a better future.

We are a superpower not only militarily but also economically. Being a superpower carries with it considerable responsibilities. While we may debate our foreign policies, no other country can manage such responsibilities as well as we do. Perhaps the only other potential candidates for the position of superpower are Russia and China. But it would not be difficult to imagine how undesirable the world would be with either one of them in such a position.

Fortunately, we do not have to worry about any military threats from Russia or China, but we do have to worry about our own economy. The largest threat not just to our world supremacy but to our way of life is a financial one. We cannot fix our financial system by working harder or collecting more taxes. But we can fix it by changing our monetary system. The US paid $222.75 billion or 6.23% of all its federal spending in interest in fiscal year 2013.*

I have suggested changing our monetary system from a debt-based system to one backed by our natural resources and infrastructure. By doing so, our treasury no longer borrows money, issues treasury notes, or pays interest. The change in our monetary policy will gradually eliminate our debt and will yield ongoing income on the money our government lends rather than on money our government borrows.

We suggested that the lottery reward many winners with a million dollars rather than a single mega-winner. We reflected on the fact that our wealth relies on a financial system that is subject to manipulation. While we cautioned about investing in gold and oil, we suggested total transparency in trading, thus eliminating the adverse effects of black-box trades. We proposed a national initiative to eliminate our dependency on fossil fuels. We argued that the paper-based US Postal Service creates waste throughout our society and suggested ways to bring it up-to-date.

We introduced the National Health and Biometric Database to store and release information about our health and DNA. We recognized that those who use this information against us can obtain the information anyway. By not having a National Health and Biometric Database, we only rob ourselves of the benefits of such a database. To ensure that our freedom is preserved, we introduced a new bill to prohibit discrimination on the basis of one's health or genetic composition. One may know my DNA just as one may know my race or gender, but one cannot use it as basis for discrimination.

We illustrated how Obamacare is a step in the right direction, but far from ideal. We suggested eliminating Medicare and Medicaid, and eliminating health insurance companies, healthcare billing, and the current wasteful process by simply having a free national healthcare system.

We discussed how if there is one war worth fighting, it is not the war on drugs, but rather a war on cancer. We recommended mandatory annual time off for employees and suggested that people stop shopping on holidays, so most people can be off work and enjoy their families.

Next I recommended that Social Security stay in its current format and maintain the retirement age for current retirees, and that the retirement age be pegged to life expectancy for future retirees. To fund it, we suggested removing the wage base for everyone but small businesses. We also introduced a new profit-sharing pension to augment the current pension plan. This pension plan would not be tax-deferred, and contributions would be a fixed percentage of a company's quarterly profits. This type of pension gives companies financial flexibility when facing tough economic times by replacing a fixed-cost pension plan with one that aligns with the company's performance.

To protect children and the elderly, we created a network of Second Homes across our nation. Second Homes would provide shelter and care for unwanted children and the needy elderly.

Next, we considered taxes. Although we kept the current progressive tax system, we simplified it and left only a few deductions. We suggested replacing the 1.45% Medicare tax with a 5–7% NHS payroll tax. For corporations, we closed tax loopholes and set a mandatory 15% minimum income tax. We also introduced an NHS corporate tax, which pays for any deficit in the NHS budget. The percentage of this tax is determined by dividing the total annual deficit by the total annual profit of US corporations.

47

Imagine

★ ★ ★ ★

We, the American people, are a family. We have over three hundred million members. One of every hundred of our family members is in prison.* More than sixteen hundred of our family members die each day from cancer. Many of us take medications for depression, anxiety, or sleep disorders, or use illicit drugs. Most of us work hard and have strong ethics, yet we do not have much to show for it. Our family has divergent views, which cannot be any further apart, on many issues, from piety to politics. We are happy, sad, depressed, angry, and mostly at war.

Nevertheless, we are a family—one of the youngest, brightest, freest, strongest, noisiest, most innovative, most philanthropic families around! But at times we can best be described as broken. Our family suffers not because of lack of resources, intelligence, or willpower, but because the capitalist track that has worked for us for so long is failing us. And that failure is because we have reached a point on the track that we neither anticipated nor prepared for. The bad news is that we are moving fast on this track, and the status quo only makes matters worse. The good news is that we can stop and even backtrack until we have it right. It would not be easy, but it is within our means.

A family prospers when each of its members is passionate and puts the welfare of the family before his or her own. It prospers when members are willing to compromise on stances that hurt the family, even if they are right. A family that puts its prejudices aside, nourishes its members, and works for the greater good will overcome all obstacles and prosper.

Let us imagine:

That every president who occupies the Oval Office is elected by popular vote.

That he or she becomes the president without needing the support of a party or a campaign budget of more than a billion dollars.

That he or she is at least a third-generation American.

That campaign promises are regarded as a contract with the people at the risk of a candidate losing his or her chance of running for reelection.

That votes are 100% reliable because proper identification is required for voting.

That we know the candidates' views not just on hot topics but on all issues important to our society.

That there is a reduction in gun-related violence because guns are biometrically operated by their registered owners.

That our politicians run for office with the sole purpose of serving our country.

That there is no threat to our democracy from multi-billionaires or mega-corporations.

That our government receives interest on the money it prints rather than pay interest, since our monetary system is no longer debt-based but backed by our natural resources and infrastructure.

That Social Security is solvent, that our retirement age is maintained, and that we have more options for retirement.

That we have a volunteer group, Freedom Watch, which provides unbiased expertise on all aspects of our society.

That we receive unbiased reporting and understand the true nature of events because the Independent Reporting Organization has ensured it.

That the Financial Transparency Service enables us to easily access information and understand how the government and government contractors spend our tax dollars.

That our Constitution is not used to protect corporations, but to protect Americans against corporations.

That the movie and gaming industries are barred from pushing gore and violence on our children.

That soft illicit drugs and prostitution are legalized, hard drugs are decriminalized, and that we can stop wasting our precious resources and worsening our problems—and that instead we use those resources to fight cancer.

That private entities are not allowed to fight our wars or run our prisons.

That we are able to reduce the number of people incarcerated in our prisons and to toughen our laws on white-collar crimes.

That capital punishment is available and carried out swiftly.

That our Postal Service is up-to-date, eliminates paper waste, and discourages the use of paper throughout our society.

That we have an initiative to eliminate our dependency on fossil fuels within fifteen to twenty years.

That all trading and stock ownership is transparent.

That our laws are simplified and kept up-to-date.

That our lotteries produce many millionaires rather than a few mega-millionaires.

That our government controls our borders and stops illegal immigration, guns, drugs, and money laundering as well as associated human-rights abuses.

That the residency status of millions of illegal immigrants is addressed.

That a bill against discrimination based on our genetic makeup is passed.

That the National Health and Biometric Database exists and provides an efficient backbone for our healthcare system.

That we have a free and efficient technology-based National Healthcare System instead of paying for the profits of private health insurance companies.

That we can reexamine our values and enjoy life's journey rather than wait for retirement.

That we celebrate our holidays by spending them with our families and loved ones and not by racing to stores and shopping malls.

That our tax system is simple enough that everyone can figure it out.

That corporations' tax loopholes are eliminated and that every company pays at least 15% of its profit in taxes.

That the legal voting age is sixteen, giving younger generations a two-year head start on political involvement.

That K–12 education is reduced to eleven years so we can become productive earlier.

That the K–10 curriculum is standardized and simplified so everyone learns what really matters.

That we offer a free three-year vocational bachelor's degree so by the time we are nineteen we know a trade.

That we learn both English and Spanish in our schools.

The premise of YFOG is to use common sense to acknowledge what is wrong with our country and reach a compromise on how to fix it. For every issue, there are experts who are for and against a proposed solution, because no solution is perfect. These imperfections allow some to see the glass half full and others to rightfully point out the empty portion of the glass. When the stakes are high, it is easy to stand on the sidelines and leave solving our problems to others who do not necessarily have our interests in mind. I believe that it is never difficult to understand a problem or its solution if we are willing to keep an open mind, think critically, and compromise.

★ Imagine ★

I started this book with a comment that expressed my perspective, and I would like to finish it in the same way. Next time that you are in disagreement with someone whose opinions you find outrageous, whose social status you consider beneath you, whose intellect you believe to be nonexistent, whose vocabulary is weak, whose accent may be offensive to you, and whom you consider inferior because of his or her skin color, keep in mind that you could have been that individual. Unless you had the opportunity to choose your parents, treat everyone as you want to be treated, respect their values, and find ways to work with them. After all, if you were that person, that is what you would have wanted.

The history of our nation is one of overcoming challenges. Our obstacles are many, but we have successfully overcome them before and we can do it again.

References

★ ★ ★ ★

Preface: The Land of the Free
The role of the CIA in the 1953 Iran coup:
    www.yfog.us/ref#61c8
    Source: www.cnn.com

Introduction: Perceptions
No source has been referenced in this chapter.

Chapter 1: The Tripod of Power
Forbes magazine's 2014 global list of billionaires:
    www.yfog.us/ref#728b
    Source: www.forbes.com

List of countries by their gross domestic product:
    www.yfog.us/ref#e19c
    Source: www.cia.gov

The O.J. Simpson case:
    www.yfog.us/ref#9c2a
    Source: law2.umkc.edu

Chapter 2: The Financial Transparency Service

United States spending in 2014:
   www.yfog.us/ref#3ad5
   Source: www.heritage.org

2011 filing for the DC chapter of Red Cross:
   www.yfog.us/ref#3cc7
   Source: foundationcenter.org

Chapte 3: Freedom Watch

No source has been referenced in this chapter.

Chapter 4: The Independent Reporting Organization

The estimate for each cable network's coverage:
   www.yfog.us/ref#ed79
   Source: tvbythenumbers.zap2it.com

CBS's 10-K for 2011:
   www.yfog.us/ref#5c51
   Source: www.sec.gov

Market capitalization of various companies:
   www.yfog.us/ref#1f70
   Source: finance.yahoo.com

Creation of the Corporation for Public Broadcasting by Congress:
   www.yfog.us/ref#816b
   Source: www.cpb.org

NPR's annual report for the year 2011:
www.yfog.us/ref#8464
Source: www.npr.org

Chapter 5: The First Amendment
Pharmaceutical companies spent $4 billion:
www.yfog.us/ref#C333
Source: www.nytimes.com

Does your doctor receive money from pharmaceutical companies?:
www.yfog.us/ref#V567
Source: projects.propublica.org

Chapter 6: Hollywood and the Gaming Industry
A description of graphic scenes from *Kingsman: The Secret Service:*
www.yfog.us/ref#y123
Source: www.imdb.com

Chapter 7: Requiring ID for Voting
No source has been referenced in this chapter.

Chapter 8: Mr. President and His Birth Certificate
Requirements to become president of United States:
www.yfog.us/ref#d375
Source: www.loc.gov

A nation of immigrants:
www.yfog.us/ref#aeb5
Source: www.pewhispanic.org

Chapter 9: Simple Majority Election

What is the Electoral College?:
> www.yfog.us/ref#9d43
> Source: www.archives.gov

Are there restrictions on whom the electors can vote for?:
> www.yfog.us/ref#6543
> Source: www.archives.gov

Why was the Electoral College created?:
> www.yfog.us/ref#9525
> Source: www.historycentral.com

Each individual vote in Wyoming counts nearly four times as much in the Electoral College as each individual vote in Texas:
> www.yfog.us/ref#a817
> Source: www.fairvote.org

National average of voters per electors:
> www.yfog.us/ref#ec99
> Source: www.fairvote.org

National Popular Vote website:
> www.yfog.us/ref#b151
> Source: www.nationalpopularvote.com

Chapter 10: Presidential Elections —
American Idol Style

132 million votes cast in *American Idol* season 11:
> www.yfog.us/ref#11b0
> Source: news.yahoo.com

129 million votes cast in 2008 presidential election:
   www.yfog.us/ref#9fee
   Source: www.washingtonpost.com

In 2012, $2.6 billion was spent on presidential election:
   www.yfog.us/ref#efc8
   Source: articles.economictimes.indiatimes.com

2012 campaign spending for congressional elections:
   www.yfog.us/ref#a1b2
   Source: www.cnn.com

Chapter 11: Politicians
No source has been referenced in this chapter.

Chapter 12: A Contract with the People
No source has been referenced in this chapter.

Chapter 13: Pit Stop 1
No source has been referenced in this chapter.

Chapter 14: Legal Age
Age of consent laws:
   www.yfog.us/ref#723b
   Source: chnm.gmu.edu

Age of consent by state:
   www.yfog.us/ref#b402
   Source: www.webistry.net/jan

US marriage law:
    www.yfog.us/ref#b888
    Source: www.usmarriagelaws.com

The minimum age to join the armed forces:
    www.yfog.us/ref#56b7
    Source: www.military.com

Quote from MIT on brain development:
    www.yfog.us/ref#66c0
    Source: hrweb.mit.edu

Chapter 15: K–10

Approximately 80% of NYC high-school grads can't read well enough for community college:
    www.yfog.us/ref#ce83
    Source: dailycaller.com

Quote from the Department of Education:
    www.yfog.us/ref#3911
    Source: www.ed.gov

Survey ranks US students 36th in the world:
    www.yfog.us/ref#961d
    Source: www.cnycentral.com

Chapter 16: English or Spanish

The number of Spanish speakers in the US:
    www.yfog.us/ref#1c5b
    Source: www.pewresearch.org

Chapter 17: National Curriculum

Siri:

www.yfog.us/ref#3baa

Source: www.apple.com

Common Core:

www.yfog.us/ref#8eea

Source: www.corestandards.org

Chapter 18: Three-Year Vocational Degree

Collective US student loan debt stands at $1.2 trillion:

www.yfog.us/ref#a786

Source: www.forbes.com

$1.2 trillion outstanding student loan debt bears 4.66% interest on average:

www.yfog.us/ref#c022

Source: www.bloomberg.com

Global higher education ranking 2010 (PDF):

www.yfog.us/ref#c5b5

Source: www.iregobservatory.org

The future of most American universities is not bright:

www.yfog.us/ref#3fb7

Source: www.economist.com

Some colleges have a little chance of surviving:

www.yfog.us/ref#983c

Source: www.economist.com

Chapter 19: Gun Politics

Maintaining a database linking bullets to guns has not been effective:

    www.yfog.us/ref#9ffc

    Source: www.freerepublic.com

Micro-stamping technology:

    www.yfog.us/ref#1484

    Source: smartgunlaws.org

Chapter 20: Illicit Drugs

A Stanford University article describes our efforts the best:

    www.yfog.us/ref#A369

    Source: https://web.stanford.edu

Anne Line Bretteville-Jensen provides a cost-benefit analysis of legalizing drugs:

    www.yfog.us/ref#5125

    Source: ash-college.ac.il

Chapter 21: Prostitution

Prostitution market's size:

    www.yfog.us/ref#22a6

    Source: www.economist.com

The reported cases of gonorrhea and rape declined when Rhode Island unintentionally decriminalized indoor prostitution between 2003 and 2009:

    www.yfog.us/ref#ee86

    Source: www.economist.com

The global market of human trafficking:
    www.yfog.us/ref#70c1
    Source: www.economist.com

10,755 cases were reported:
    www.yfog.us/ref#32e1
    Source: traffickingresourcecenter.org

Chapter 22: Private Prisons

They spent $45 million in campaign donations:
    www.yfog.us/ref#13c8
    Source: thinkprogress.org

Yahoo report on immigration policy on private prisons:
    www.yfog.us/ref#5e7d
    Source: finance.yahoo.com

An excerpt from the annual report by a top private prison:
    www.yfog.us/ref#6za2
    Source: 2010 Annual Report on Form 10-K

Two-thirds of released prisoners were rearrested within three years of release:
    www.yfog.us/ref#c583
    Source: www.nij.gov

25 cents an hour:
    www.yfog.us/ref#74e0
    Source: www.globalresearch.ca

PRRS:
    www.yfog.us/ref#8d41
    Source: www.montgomerycountymd.gov

Chapter 23: Capital Punishment

The cost of maintaining an inmate:

www.yfog.us/ref#7c4a

Source: www.mountain-news.com

Chapter 24: White-Collar Crimes

As a result of the 2008 financial meltdown, only one banker was sentenced:

www.yfog.us/ref#7a43

Source: www.nytimes.com

Chapter 25: One-Time Parole

In the United States, one out of every hundred adults is incarcerated:

www.yfog.us/ref#dc41

Source: www.economist.com

Out of about 71,000 juveniles in jails and prisons, around 11,600 are imprisoned for technical violations:

www.yfog.us/ref#7caf

Source: www.economist.com

Chapter 26: Border Control and Immigration

Millions of illegal immigrants:

www.yfog.us/ref#6994

Source: www.migrationpolicy.org

In 1970 and 2000, there were 9.6 million:

www.yfog.us/ref#8f29

Source: www.migrationpolicy.org

10,000 Chinese women gave birth in the US:
    www.yfog.us/ref#7632
    Source: money.cnn.com

When illegal immigrants become legal, they overwhelmingly
vote for the Democratic Party:
    www.yfog.us/ref#db8b
    Source: www.pewresearch.org

Chapter 27: Sunset Clause
No source has been referenced in this chapter.

Chapter 28: Pit Stop 2
No source has been referenced in this chapter.

Chapter 29: Capping Capitalism
Forbes's list of billionaires:
    www.yfog.us/ref#f327
    Source: www.forbes.com

We taxed income over $200,000 at 94% in 1944:
    www.yfog.us/ref#Z222
    Source: bradfordtaxinstitute.com

Chapter 30: Banking and the US Monetary System
Federal Reserve monetary policy:
    www.yfog.us/ref#fcc8
    Source: federalreserve.gov

"A dollar in 1971 was worth less than 19 cents in 2012":
    www.yfog.us/ref#dc8b
    Source: www.forbes.com

Thomas Jefferson's quote:
    www.yfog.us/ref#b01b
    Source: www.goodreads.com

The top 65 global banks:
    www.yfog.us/ref#6866
    Source: www.relbanks.com

The bank rate:
    www.yfog.us/ref#871a
    Source: www.reuters.com

Bloomberg won a court case:
    www.yfog.us/ref#bb03
    Source: www.bloomberg.com

4.4 million of our homes were foreclosed upon:
    www.yfog.us/ref#19c6
    Source: www.businessinsider.com

There is $1.2 trillion in outstanding student loans:
    www.yfog.us/ref#4089
    Source: www.huffingtonpost.com

The bank rate:
    www.yfog.us/ref#2d58
    Source: www.bloomberg.com

In 2013, we paid $222.75 billion in interest:
www.yfog.us/ref#c944
Source: www.pewresearch.org

Chapter 31: The Lottery
No source has been referenced in this chapter.

Chapter 32: Transparent Trading
Black-box trading was responsible for one-third of all trading in 2009:
www.yfog.us/ref#340d
Source: www.economist.com

Goldman Sachs's rapid-fire stock-and-commodities-trading software:
www.yfog.us/ref#8989
Source: www.bloomberg.com

Chapter 33: Energy and Oil
World energy sources (PDF):
www.yfog.us/ref#c99c
Source: www.iea.org

The link between energy consumption and standard of living:
www.yfog.us/ref#50cd
Source: osqar.suncor.com

Chapter 34: Post Office

About the USPS:
www.yfog.us/ref#5bcf
Source: about.usps.com

The USPS 2012 annual report:
www.yfog.us/ref#b204
Source: about.usps.com

Chapter 35: National Health and Biometric Database

Who can legally access our medical records?:
www.yfog.us/ref#da1c
Source: patients.about.com

Chapter 36: Genetic Discrimination Bill

No source has been referenced in this chapter.

Chapter 37: SAM

Apple's Siri:
www.yfog.us/ref#1f25
Source: www.apple.com

IBM's Watson:
www.yfog.us/ref#1b2e
Source: www.ibm.com

A joint venture of IBM, WellPoint, and Memorial Sloan Kettering Cancer Center (MSK):
www.yfog.us/ref#1315
Source: www.mskcc.org

On another front, global medical wearables, a $2.9 billion market in 2014, will grow to $8.3 billion in revenue by 2019:
    www.yfog.us/ref#3c98
    Source: mordorintelligence.com

Wearables currently have a broad range of functions:
    www.yfog.us/ref#3ee3
    Source: vandrico.com

It would take 160 hours a week for a doctor to keep up with these advancements:
    www.yfog.us/ref#9d6a
    Source: www.economist.com

Chapter 38: National Healthcare System

Before Obamacare, there were 48 million uninsured people in America:
    www.yfog.us/ref#2588
    Source: kaiserhealthnews.org

In 2014, 6.8 million enrolled in a plan through healthcare.gov:
    www.yfog.us/ref#34e9
    Source: obamacarefacts.com

This translates to around $38.25 billion in revenue for health insurance companies:
    www.yfog.us/ref#3b63
    Source: hd.egain.com

Employer mandate:
    www.yfog.us/ref#fc60
    Source: obamacarefacts.com

Individual mandate:
　　www.yfog.us/ref#4d8e
　　Source: www.government-health-insurance.com

The Supreme Court has recognized this penalty as taxes:
　　www.yfog.us/ref#9d00
　　Source: www.nytimes.com

The NHS would sponsor internships much as Medicare does today:
　　www.yfog.us/ref#ce3b
　　Source: www.aamc.org

$884 billion in revenues in 2013:
　　www.yfog.us/ref#36ee
　　Source: healthcareforamericanow.org

Chapter 39: The War on ~~Drugs~~ Cancer

The death toll from cancer in 2015 alone (589,430) is higher than the number of Americans who died in World War I (116,516), World War II (405,399), Vietnam (58,209), and Iraq (4,489) combined (584,613).

Statistics on wars:
　　www.yfog.us/ref#dcf2
　　Source: www.militaryfactory.com

Statistics on cancer:
　　www.yfog.us/ref#37c0
　　Source: www.cancer.org

Survival rate:
   www.yfog.us/ref#be08
   Source: www.ovaconline.org

Cancer statistics:
   www.yfog.us/ref#6d24
   Source: www.cancer.org

The cost of cancer:
   www.yfog.us/ref#7252
   Source: www.ovaconline.org

Memorial Sloan Kettering Cancer Center:
   www.yfog.us/ref#f6aa
   Source: www.mskcc.org

Chapter 40: Work to Live, Not Live to Work

Two-fifths of us leave our paid vacation unused:
   www.yfog.us/ref#b258
   Source: www.huffingtonpost.com

FMLA:
   www.yfog.us/ref#caf8
   Source: www.dol.gov

Chapter 41: National Holidays

No source has been referenced in this chapter.

Chapter 42: Social Security and Retirement

Issues facing Social Security:
   www.yfog.us/ref#4c4f
   Source: www.forbes.com

Social security deficit in 2014:
 www.yfog.us/ref#a940
 Source: www.ssa.gov

Social Security consists of three programs:
 www.yfog.us/ref#d53a
 Source: www.heritage.org

Full retirement age:
 www.yfog.us/ref#f996
 Source: www.motherjones.com

Wage base:
 www.yfog.us/ref#3b0a
 Source: www.ssa.gov

Calculate your Social Security benefits:
 www.yfog.us/ref#469e
 Source: www.ssa.gov

Average life expectancy:
 www.yfog.us/ref#7010
 Source: web.stanford.edu

Historical average life expectancy:
 www.yfog.us/ref#a9a9
 Source: www.ssa.gov

Possibility of people living to 150:
 www.yfog.us/ref#20a5
 Source: www.slate.com

Cutting benefits:
    www.yfog.us/ref#5d8a
    Source: www.washingtonpost.com

A dollar in 1971 was worth less than 19 cents in 2012:
    www.yfog.us/ref#5e7a
    Source: www.forbes.com

When early retirement age is increased by 5 years:
    www.yfog.us/ref#f09b
    Source: www.cdc.gov

Info on 401(k)s:
    www.yfog.us/ref#16ab
    Source: www.irs.gov

401(k)s are the most popular retirement plans offered by companies, valued at $4.4 trillion:
    www.yfog.us/ref#798f
    Source: www.ici.org

Chapter 43: Second Home

1.6 million homeless children:
    www.yfog.us/ref#181e
    Source: www.familyhomelessness.org

Chapter 44: Morality, Legality, Normality

The experiment with a daycare where parents were fined if they were late to pick up their children, as discussed in the book *Freakonomics*:
    www.yfog.us/ref#f216
    Source: freakonomics.com

Chapter 45: Government and Taxes

The US budget for the year 2015 is $3.9 trillion:
www.yfog.us/ref#961e
Source: www.whitehouse.gov

The market cap of the 12 largest US banks:
www.yfog.us/ref#628e
Source: www.relbanks.com

Top 20 companies by market caps:
www.yfog.us/ref#86f4
Source: www.theonlineinvestor.com

One theory is that our justice department:
www.yfog.us/ref#5490
Source: www.nytimes.com

Over 30 million commercial flights:
www.yfog.us/ref#79f5
Source: www.cnn.com

The cost of Healthcare.gov, the official administration website for Obamacare, could be above $600 million:
www.yfog.us/ref#77f0
Source: www.washingtonpost.com

The history of WebMD:
www.yfog.us/ref#3511
Source: www.fundinguniverse.com

WebMD market cap:
www.yfog.us/ref#6021
Source: finance.yahoo.com

WebMD unique visitors per month:
   www.yfog.us/ref#910c
   Source: investor.shareholder.com

Estate tax exemption:
   www.yfog.us/ref#252b
   Source: www.bankrate.com

In addition, charitable, educational, medical, political gifts, and gifts to spouses are exempt:
   www.yfog.us/ref#5f72
   Source: www.bankrate.com

An employer pays $4,266 on average to cover an employee; while an employee pays $1,118:
   www.yfog.us/ref#5399
   Source: kff.org

The annual out-of-pocket expense per household is $3,301:
   www.yfog.us/ref#dac8
   Source: www.bankrate.com

An annual median individual income of $28,155:
   www.yfog.us/ref#b54e
   Source: quickfacts.census.gov

Chapter 46: Pit Stop 3

The US paid $222.75 billion, or 6.23% of all its federal spending, in interest in fiscal year 2013:
   www.yfog.us/ref#4ded
   Source: www.pewresearch.org

Chapter 47: Imagine

One of every hundred of our family members is in prison. According to economist, there were 2.4 million people in prisons, 721,654 in jails, and 22,870 as immigrations detainee as of June 2012. That is 3,144,524 or one percent of 316,100,000 US population:

http://www.yfog.us/ref#7c7c

Source: www.economist.com

About the Author

★ ★ ★ ★

Matt Tabrizi, the son of a family of merchants, left his native Iran for the United States shortly after the revolution there in 1979. After studying biology at Virginia Commonwealth University, he began a career in the Information Technology sector. Since then, he's held leadership positions in a variety of fields, focusing on business management and developing startups. He lives with his loving wife and two sons in the suburbs of Washington, DC.

www.ingramcontent.com/pod-product-compliance
Lightning Source LLC
Chambersburg PA
CBHW060252100426
42742CB00011B/1728

* 9 7 8 0 9 9 9 6 2 1 0 0 0 3 *